The Sailor in the Wardrobe

ALSO BY HUGO HAMILTON

The Speckled People
Surrogate City
The Last Shot
The Love Test
Headbanger
Sad Bastard

The Sailor in the Wardrobe

HUGO HAMILTON

FOURTH ESTATE • London

Special thanks to Petra Eggers, Nina Härte,
Rainer Milzkott, and also to Arcadia in Potsdam

First published in Great Britain in 2006 by
Fourth Estate
An imprint of HarperCollins*Publishers*
77–85 Fulham Palace Road
London W6 8JB
www.4thestate.co.uk

Copyright © Hugo Hamilton 2006

2

The right of Hugo Hamilton to be identified as the author of
this work has been asserted by him in accordance with the
Copyright, Designs and Patents Act 1988

A catalogue record for this book is
available from the British Library

HB ISBN-13 978-0-00-719217-5
HB ISBN-10 0-00-719217-7

TPB ISBN-13 978-0-00-722444-9
TPB ISBN-10 0-00-722444-3

Set in Garamond 3

Printed in Great Britain by Clays Ltd, St Ives plc

for Máire

Die Zerrissenheit ist unsere Identität.
Disconnectedness is our identity.

Hans Magnus Enzensberger

One

People say you're born innocent, but it's not true. You inherit all kinds of things that you can do nothing about. You inherit your identity, your history, like a birthmark that you can't wash off. We have our Irish history and our German history, like an original sin. We are born with our heads turned back, but my mother says we have to face into the future now. You have to earn your own innocence, she says. You have to grow up and become innocent.

The front door of our house is wide open. She has opened all the windows as well, to let in the air. There is no wind, only the long net curtains in the front room floating a little and the hum of summer all around the house. The floor has been polished and we have the solstice shining along the hallway. Once, my father brought us up to Newgrange in the car and told us about the winter solstice, how the sun reaches right into the megalithic tomb at Christmas and lights up the inner chamber. He says it's like a piece of knowledge entering into the mind. Now we have the first summer solstice shining through our house, lighting up the shadowed places. For a few moments, the sun is reflected against one of the top windows on the red-bricked terrace across the road and beams right in through the hallway. It bounces off the wooden floor and off the carved oak trunk and shines right through into the kitchen at the back. It doesn't last long, but while it does, there is a glint on every door handle, on vases, on picture frames, so bright that it makes you almost blind. All you can see is the white shape of the door frame and the fanlight.

On the roof of the breakfast room, my father is looking after the bees. I go outside to help him and watch him stepping carefully around the hives. We're like two astronauts out there, standing on top of a strange planet with square bee-keeping cages around our heads, working in silence. He signals to me with his big glove and I hand him the smoker, and then the stainless steel lever so he can lift out the frames to make sure the bees are not thinking of swarming. The bees don't like to be exposed to the light. They cling to the frames like a moving beard, listening to the restless thoughts in his mind. I can hear their tiny voices in thousands, like one strong, fizzing growl, as if they're already planning to kill him. For the moment there is a truce, and we close up the hives again. We put away the bee-keeping gear and he tells me to come down into the front room.

'There's something I want you to know,' he says.

He closes the door. The atmosphere is solemn. My mother is already sitting down, waiting.

'I think you're old enough to hear this,' he says. He wants me to know what happened when the war was over and my mother was trying to get home. I have been chosen to receive this message from the past, a story about the British, one that we have to sit down for.

My mother talks about the phosphor bombs that rained down on the cities and about the final defeat, about the last shot being fired and the time of liberation, when everybody was finally on their way home. She remembers the feeling of freedom that was in the air that summer, like the smell of grass. She had to make her way back from Czechoslovakia where everybody was still running away from the Russians. She was on a German army truck with the Russian tanks no more than half a kilometre behind, cutting across the fields to try and head them off. In the end she got away only because of the mud everywhere and the roads so full of people that the Russians couldn't catch them. At the border, the German soldiers changed out of their uniforms and became civilians again. She remembers seeing a mound of helmets and guns lying beside the road. She was lucky because she cycled through the Fichtel mountains with an officer who had secretly decided to hold on to his gun and then saved her life. All the way down to Nuremberg they had to take the highest roads by day and hide in the forests by night. It was the start of a beautiful hot summer, she says, but the officer was already married, so they had to say goodbye to each other and she continued on her way home, getting a lift with the American soldiers back towards the Rhineland.

Then we come to the part of the story that my father is waiting for. He has a frown on his forehead and his lips are pushed forward, listening to every word. My mother explains how, at the British checkpoint, she was brought into a compound where everybody was being processed. The men were separated from the women. She had to show her papers and answer questions about where she had been and what she had done with her life. The men were taken away and the officer in charge ordered all the women to line up outside. Around sixty to eighty women in all, my mother says, young and old, standing in a line while the officer walked up and down with a clipboard under his arm that had all their names on it. With the strong sunlight in their eyes, they could hardly see much more of him than the black outline of his uniform. There were trucks going past and a smell of diesel and dust in the air. There was an airfield somewhere close by too, because they could hear planes landing and taking off in the distance.

The officer then ordered them to undress down to the waist. An interpreter shouted out the order, but most of them understood the words in English. It didn't look like a medical examination and the women looked around at each other, afraid of what was going to happen next. They obeyed and stood semi-naked with the trucks going by and the soldiers staring at them, whistling from up high as they passed. Some of the soldiers shouted things out, but their accents were hard to understand, even when they used German words like 'Fräulein'.

My mother refused to undress. She had not always obeyed Hitler either. The officer soon came over and began to shout at her. He had a red face and maybe he was too hot inside his uniform, because he began tapping his clipboard against his leg until one of the women told her not to make so much of a fuss or she would get them all into trouble.

I don't like hearing this story because it gives me the hurt mind. My mother undressed to the waist like the others, but as soon as the officer turned away, she pulled her dress back up again. The officer was angry that she would not surrender like everyone else. He marched straight over and pulled her dress down with his hand. The soldiers on the trucks waiting to leave the compound let out a big cheer. She could not see them against the sunlight, but she could smell their cigarette smoke. When the officer moved on again, she pulled her dress up

4

to stop them staring and making remarks about German women. But he returned and ripped her dress down once more, shouting into her face in English, with the men on the trucks giving another big cheer. She had to give in finally because the women beside her told her it wasn't worth it, the Germans had lost the war and the British had won.

'Just let them see how beautiful we are,' one of the women remarked.

Then my mother starts laughing. She says it was a German joke, because the woman who said it was very old, with wrinkled skin and not much for men to look at. She remembers how they all started laughing, even though most of them were ashamed and hungry and weak from walking, worried about what would happen next. They were worried about getting home, worried about what was left after the bombing and who was still alive, and even though they laughed quietly with their shoulders as if they had nothing more to lose, the real joke was on the German women now, standing half-naked in the sun with the whistles echoing in their ears as the trucks came and went. They had to suffer the humiliation of being defeated women, standing for ages in the burning heat with their hands down by their sides until some of the women began to faint and they all got a very nice sunburn before being let go, she says.

My father stands up and goes over to put his arm around her shoulder. I can hear his voice shaking as he speaks.

'They shamed her,' he says.

My mother is smiling now, trying to say that she's lucky to be alive and it could have been much worse, like what happened to women in the east who were killed by the Germans, women who had all their dignity taken away from them, women who went to their death along with their children. Women who sang songs to their children at the last minute to make them less worried before they died in the concentration camps.

'The Germans shamed themselves,' she says. 'Don't forget that.'

But my father will not let it go. He is angry and sad at the same time. I can see his chin quivering. He speaks as if my mother has become part of Irish history now. He admires her for refusing to undress for the British and says she has the rebel heart. He wishes he could have been there to defend her, but it's too late and too long ago and there's nothing he can do about it any more except not to allow anything British under his roof. All he can do is stop English words coming into our house and drive everything British out of Ireland. He is still trying to protect her from this humiliation and wants me to remember that my mother's family had been against the Nazis all along. Her uncle lost his job as Lord Mayor for not joining the party. Her sister Marianne turned her guest house in Salzburg into a safe haven during the war, hiding a Jewish woman who went around dressed as a Catholic nun. My mother disobeyed orders so that she could bring food to Salzburg and was arrested as a deserter, then sent to the east in a locked train carriage with a young boy soldier who was chained to the seat.

'The British have no right to pass judgment on anyone,' he says. There are other things to remember as well, things to do with Irish history, things that are still going on in Northern Ireland. He takes my mother's hand. He has tears in his eyes and he can hardly speak any more.

'They should look into their own hearts,' he says.

My mother smiles and says it's time to walk away from the hurt. It's the time of forgiveness and peace. It's time to imagine the dead people back to life again in our memory. It's time to grow up and become innocent.

'We just want to give you a conscience,' she says finally.

After that the room is silent for a long time. My father takes off his glasses and wipes his eyes with the upper part of his wrist. It's hard to look at them, sitting together side by side, unable to get away from the past. Maybe that's why people have to pass things on to their children, so they can be freed from it themselves. I feel the weight of all this information in my chest because it's the story of my mother being shamed. It's like a blinding solstice entering into my head. I am the boy who was born with his head turned back and I can't stop thinking of my mother, standing in the glare of the sunlight after the war, with nothing to say. I am the son of a German woman who was shamed in front of the world, and the son of an Irishman who is refusing to surrender to the British.

These are things I need to forget, things I don't want to think about any more. I want to have no past behind me, no conscience and no memory. I want to get away from my home and my family and my history.

When I'm finally allowed to leave, I walk out the front door into the sunshine. I take my bike and feel the breeze coming in from the sea on my way down to the harbour. I pass by men in overalls painting the blue railings along the seafront. I hear them talking to each other, banging and scraping off the rust. I smell the paint and the cigarettes they smoke, like a new colour in the air. At the harbour, my friend Packer has got me a job working with an old fisherman. Nobody asks where I come from. It's just me and Packer and the other lads working for Dan

Turley, sitting on the trellis outside his shed on the pier, listening to the faraway sound of the radio and laughing at our own jokes. Dan Turley lying on his bunk inside the shed with his white cap right down over his eyes and us sitting outside in the sun with the painted signs behind us. Big white lettering on a blue background saying: fresh mackerel, lobster for sale, boats for hire, trips around the island.

People come from all over the place to buy fish and lobster. Some people hire out the boats to go fishing and others go for the pleasure trip. When they come back in, we have to tie up the boat, calculate how many hours they've been out, take the money and enter it into the book with the stub of a pencil on a string. All the boats have different names, like *Sarah Jane* and *Printemps*. Sometimes we have to go up on the rocks at the back of the shed with the binoculars, to make sure none of the boats are in difficulty. Sometimes we have to go out to rescue them when the engine fails. Couples going out to the island to lie around on the grass. Groups of them going out thinking it's warm and only realizing when they get out there how breezy it can be. Then you see one of the women coming back shivering, wrapped up in a man's jacket, maybe even pale and seasick because they're not used to being out on the water. Sometimes it's the opposite, when they go out in raincoats and come back all pink and sunburned down one side with half a red face. Sometimes you look out and it's raining in one part of the bay while the sun is still shining straight down in another part, like a desk-lamp on the water. Sometimes the sea is rough and nobody can go out at all because the red flag is up. And sometimes people only come to look, men walking their dogs, women wearing sunglasses on top of their heads, nurses from the nursing home over-looking the harbour bringing the old people down in their wheelchairs to stare at the boats.

It's the harbour of forgetting and never looking back.

This summer I'm going to escape and earn my own innocence. It's goodbye to the past and goodbye to war and resentment. It's goodbye to the killing news on the radio, goodbye to funerals and goodbye to crying. It's goodbye to flags and countries. Goodbye to the shame and goodbye to the blame and goodbye to the hurt mind.

Two

It looked as if everything had stopped moving. You could feel the boat drifting and hear the water making all kinds of swallowing noises underneath. Everything was rocking, but it looked like we were stuck in the same spot all the time, because the sun was shining again, like a thousand liquid mirrors flashing across the water. Everything was white and blank and you could not even see the land any more, as if the country we came from had disappeared and we now had no country to go back to. You knew where it was, right in front of you. You could imagine the shape of it in your head – the hill, the harbour and the church spires. You could hear lots of familiar sounds coming from the shore – a motorbike, a train going into the city. There were men drilling on roadworks somewhere, except that it didn't sound like drilling at all to us, more like somebody ringing a small bell. Everything was far away and it was just me and Dan, drifting and jigging the fishing lines up and down, not saying very much to each other, as if there was some sort of fisherman's law of silence in the boat. Sooner or later we could see that we were not standing still at all and that the tide had already taken us close to the island. Dan muttered something and we pulled in the lines. The boat bounced across the waves and the spray came over the bow, wetting my bare arms, until we came level with the harbour again and he cut the engine. We threw out the lines and drifted once more, listening to the water giggling underneath, until we hit a shoal of mackerel and the boat was suddenly full of flapping.

Then I heard a shout coming from the shore.

'Turley.'

His name, nothing more. I looked to see if he had heard it too. Along the top of the rocks there was somebody standing with the advantage of the sun behind him, but we could see nothing and the shout could have come from any of the caves along the coast that looked like open mouths. It could have come from the small stone ruin or from any of the dark windows of a derelict house on the cliff. It was just the one shout, no more. Somebody who knew him. A hostile call that hung in the air over the water and would not go away, as if somebody wanted him to know that he was being watched and that they had not forgotten, that's all.

I know there is no place to hide from your memory and no place to hide from your own name. It will come after you, following you down the street, on the bus, even out in the boat. Your own name following you like a curse. Packer told me that Dan Turley comes from Derry and that he's got enemies, but we don't know much more than that because he never talks about himself. He's the man who never looks back, the man who wants to forget his own name and where he came from, like me.

My father and mother taught us how to forget and how to remember. My father still makes speeches at the breakfast table and my mother still cuts out pictures and articles from the newspapers to put into her diary when she has time. She wants to make sure that we remember how we grew up and don't repeat what happened to her in

Germany. She wants everything to be fixed and glued into her book. Our history and the history of the world all mixed together. There is a lock of blond hair on one page and a picture of Martin Luther King on the next. School reports and pictures of tanks on the streets of Prague facing each other.

Whenever we had nightmares in our family, she would get up in the middle of the night to take out a piece of paper and coloured pencils. Here, draw the nightmare, she would say. Once you put it down on paper, you will never have to dream about it again. So we would sit up in bed with the light on, rubbing our eyes and drawing whatever it was that frightened us. Sometimes I couldn't remember what the nightmare was. My fingers were so weak with sleep that I couldn't even hold the pencil or push it down onto the paper. But she would wait patiently with her arm around me, until the bad thing was drawn and coloured in. Look, she would then say, it's there in your drawing and we can put it away. Now we have un-remembered it and we can go back to sleep again.

Our family is a factory of remembering and forgetting. My mother's diary is full of secrets and nightmares. There's a drawing by my sister Maria of a wolf with green teeth preventing her from getting down to my mother at the bottom of the stairs. There's a picture of my brother Franz in one window of the house and everybody else in separate windows of the same house, unable to speak to each other or hear each other calling, because each room has a different colour and a different language. There's a picture of a river coming through the front door with lots of people that we don't know on boats sailing along the hall, speaking English. There were nightmares in Irish and nightmares in German. Nightmares in English that could only be drawn without words. Family nightmares and world nightmares. I once drew the picture of a Jewish man who had his beard ripped off and his chin was all red, because my mother told me that story and I couldn't stop thinking about it. There's a drawing of Roger Casement being buried in Glasnevin. Another drawing of the Berlin wall and people trying to escape through the windows of their houses, throwing their suitcases and their children down first.

Sometimes we had to draw the nightmare and also the solution. Maria at the bottom of the stairs in my mother's arms, and the wolf locked in the bathroom. My sister Bríd standing at the window getting lots of good blue air into her lungs instead of bad red air. Nightmares about my mother not being in the same country as us. At one time, my drawings were all full of pigs and chickens and farmers facing in one direction. All the smoke and all the flags were flying to the left until one night, when my mother discovered that she was the only person looking the other way, to the right. She told me to turn her around and then everything was fine, with all of us facing in the same direction, all in the same country again.

There were so many nightmares in our house that my mother must have been up all night sometimes. As soon as one bad thing was down on paper, something new would get into our heads. The more we drew our night-mares, the more we made up new ones. There are night drawings of skeletons, snakes, spiders, lions, walls with eyes, doors with teeth, stairs with massive earthquake cracks opening up on our way to bed. We used up every monster there was, my mother says, and there could hardly be any more nightmares left for us, but still we invented more. And downstairs at night, I know my

13

father and mother were busy with their own nightmares. My father in the front room trying to write articles for the papers and thinking of new inventions that would make Ireland a better place. My mother in the kitchen at the back, putting her German secrets into her diary along with ours.

It was the nightmare factory. Other families were obsessed with sport, or music, or practising Irish dancing. We grew up dreaming about things that happened and things that had not happened yet and things we wished had never happened. By drawing everything down on paper, we developed a special talent for inventing fears and nightmares. We became the nightmare artists.

At some point we all started dreaming fire. A timber yard went up in flames in Dublin one night and you could see the firemen on ladders directing the water across the walls. An oil tanker on fire and the whole sea covered in flames. Trees on fire in Vietnam. Blazing cars in Northern Ireland. A man named Jan Palach set himself on fire on Wenceslas Square in Prague. My mother remembered seeing lots of things on fire with her own eyes in Germany during the war. She remembered the synagogue in Kempen on fire and no firemen helping to put it out. So then it was drawings of buildings on fire, prams on fire, a doll's house on fire. Now it's buses burning in Belfast and you think there's almost no point in fixing anything down on paper any more, because it keeps coming back again and again on the TV every night, right in front of your eyes.

All over the world, there is trouble on the streets now and trouble inside the houses. Civil rights demonstrations. People marching with placards and throwing stones at the police. At dinner, my father slaps his hand on the table and says things are changing in Northern Ireland at last, things that were left unfinished for years. He points at the TV and says he can't wait for the future when things will be just like they were in the old days before the British.

You can see them throwing stones and petrol bombs at the police. Everybody talking about a place called the Bogside in Derry where the police were firing tear gas at the people in the street and you saw the crowd of protesters, some of them like cowboys with handkerchiefs over their mouths and noses, picking up the gas canisters and throwing them back. My father says it must be against the Geneva convention to use CS gas on people in the street, where there could be children and old people nearby with bad chests and lung conditions. At the battle of the Bogside, you saw them throwing petrol bombs down from the roof of the flats. The people of Derry were winning because the women start factories of petrol bombs and there was an endless supply that kept raining down onto the police. You saw a policeman on fire, screaming and kicking the flames away off his legs. Other policemen coming to help him, beating the fire off with their shields. Eventually the police lost the battle and the British army was called in. My father said the picture was complete now with the four allies from the Second World War still doing the same thing, as if they could not get out of the habit. It was French troops in Algeria, Russian troops in Prague, American troops in Vietnam, and now the British troops in Northern Ireland. We heard Jack Lynch saying that we could no longer stand idly by and watch Irish people getting hurt again. I even made a petrol bomb myself one day, because I was working in a garage at the time. But then I had nothing much to throw it at, so I just lit it and watched the earth on fire in the lane at the back.

When the British soldiers first arrived in Belfast, the Catholic people thought it was a great liberation because at least they were no longer going to be ruled by their Protestant neighbours. We saw pictures of women on the streets, handing out cups of tea to the soldiers and saying they were welcome. But that didn't last long and very soon, the British soldiers were despised even more than their neighbours. The same women who had given them tea were seen kneeling down in the streets, banging dustbin lids as the soldiers went by in Saracen jeeps. The army of occupation, they were called now, and you could hear the sound of dustbin lids echoing all over the city like a long shout, like the curse of history following them wherever they went through the streets. One day I came home and saw my mother banging the dustbin lid on the granite step in front of the house. I could hear it echo along the street and it looked like she was carrying out a solitary protest of her own. When I asked her if she was doing it against the British, she laughed out loud and kept repeating it all evening, because no such thing had ever even entered into her head and she was only banging the lid to try and knock the snails off.

And now the long shout was coming after Dan Turley. I heard it very clearly, as if it was right beside us, or above us. Just one shout, like an accusation that would not go away. Dan's surname left hanging in the air all around us. I knew how threatening it was to hear your own name being shouted out like this by some invisible voice. Your own name like the worst insult in the world, following you down the street like a million banging dustbin lids.

We had struck a shoal and were pulling in the mackerel. Dozens of them, leaping into the boat as if they were surrendering. The boat was full of slapping as the fish jumped around inside the metal box. I once asked Dan what it was like for mackerel. Was it the same as drowning for us or was it more like getting drunk, suffocating with too much oxygen, like when you breathe in fast and get dizzy? But he said nothing. He never says much. He doesn't even call me by name. He just mutters and sometimes you have to guess what he's saying in his Northern accent. I know very little about him. I know he's an old man, over seventy. But he doesn't want conversations about where you're from and what age you are and how a mackerel feels when he's dying on the bottom of the boat, staring at people's shoes up close. All he told me once was that mackerel never stop moving. They can't stay still. They're on the run all the time, travelling at thirty miles an hour underwater without stopping.

Dan ignored the shout and pretended it wasn't his name. Maybe he had heard this kind of phantom shout many times before, but then he must have lost his concentration, because the line suddenly slipped out of his hand and ran out across the gunwale. He tried to catch it, but a hook buried itself deep, right in between thumb and forefinger.

'Hook,' he said through his teeth and I saw the blood in his hand.

Ever since I started working at the harbour, I have been dreaming about hooks in jaws. Hooks in eyes, hooks in every part of your body. Hook torture and hook crucifixion. Maybe I should have got up one night and drawn it down on paper so that it would go away, because now it was happening in front of my eyes.

He was helpless for a moment, staring down at his hand, gripping it with the other hand, trying to squeeze out the pain with his thumb and forefinger, as if it was the sound of his own name that hurt so much. The blood was already leaking into his palm, mixing in with the blood of mackerel and fish scales. Outside the boat, the mackerel were tugging at the line, swimming around in circles, trying to get away and digging the hook deeper. I knew what to do. I pulled in my line and threw it across the floor of the boat with the fish still on their hooks. There was no time to do the same with his, so I got the filleting knife and cut it. The remaining mackerel were released and swirled away on their hooks, shackled to each other for ever by this piece of lost line, swimming down and sideways as if they couldn't agree where to go at all.

He examined his hand and started swivelling the hook around, forcing more blood out and making everything worse. Then he held his hand towards me. I didn't trust myself and felt his hand shaking as I tried moving the hook around slowly like a surgeon to see if I could reverse it out without doing any more damage.

'Pull the fucken' thing,' he growled.

I had to extract it quickly. Pretend it was another mackerel. I pulled as fast as I could, but it tore a hole and left a bit of loose flesh dangling. He took in a deep breath and narrowed his eyes. I let go of his hand and saw blood on my fingers. Then I dropped the hook on the floor of the boat with the soggy, brown cigarette butts, because we were already very close to the island, almost on top of the rocks, and there was no time to lose. I could see the ribbons of black seaweed waving and the shape of the rocks, like large, luminous green creatures swimming underneath, waiting for us. He moved aside so that I could start the engine as fast as possible. He sat holding his clenched hands, as if he was praying, with the blood running into the sleeve of his jacket. I turned the boat around and the engine scraped across the back of one of the rocks beneath us. It made an underwater groan, but I managed to steer away from danger and head towards the harbour.

On our way back, the sun disappeared behind a cloud, so I could see everything very clearly without holding my hand up over my eyes. The land came back into view, but there was nobody to be seen on top of the rocks. I looked at the fish on the bottom of the boat. Most of them were rigid by now, but one or two of them were brought back to life again as the boat bounced across the water, wriggling fiercely one last time before going quiet again. Dan reached his hand out over the side of the boat and washed it. He stared across the water behind us, dreaming with his eyes open. He didn't want to talk about it and I knew he didn't want me to tell anyone. When we got back to the harbour, he left me to tie up the boat and carry everything in, while he got out and walked away with his hands in the pockets of his jacket. He was not in a rush. He walked back across the pier and disappeared inside the shed as if nothing had happened.

The harbour is a place of nightmares, but it's where I want to be. I love the sight of the wide open bay and the clouds, like big handwriting in the sky. I love the moon shining on the water at night, like a soft, powdery white light drifting across the world. I belong to the sea, like my grandfather, John Hamilton, the sailor with the soft eyes who got locked into the wardrobe by my father. I know he lost his life when he fell on board a British navy ship during the First World War. And after the Irish liberated their country from British rule, he disappeared, because my father wants Ireland to be fully Irish and thinks his own father betrayed his country. When we were small, we got trapped in the wardrobe along with the sailor once and had to be rescued. I am the same age now as my grandfather was when he joined the navy, so I'm stepping into his shoes. I work on the boats and go out fishing like his people did in Glandore, on the coast of West Cork. Sometimes I sneak upstairs to the wardrobe while my father is at work and look at the photograph of John Hamilton in his sailor's tunic. I wonder if I look like him. I want to be a sailor and travel all over the world like he did before he died. I'm going to become my own grandfather. I'm going to take his name and help him to escape out of the wardrobe.

Three

On my way home from the harbour, I see people going swimming with towels rolled up under their arms. The tide is in and I see them changing, leaving their clothes in bundles on the blue benches. Girls doing the Houdini trick behind their big towels and coming out in their swimsuits. I stop for a moment to watch them jumping off the rocks, yelping and splashing as they go in. They swim around to the steps and come up all wet and skinny, then do the whole thing all over again. Girls ganging up on the boys and them all going in together. One of the boys on the diving board pretending to die with a guitar in his hands, singing 'I've got that loving feeling' as he falls backwards with a big splash. I know that as you go into the water like this, there is a moment when you stop moving altogether and just hang in the same spot underwater without breathing, surrounded by silence and air bubbles before you begin to move back up towards the surface. You feel no gravity. You become weightless.

After dinner every evening, my father is sawing and hammering. This time he's building a big music centre. I've seen the plans, with separate sections for the turntable and the amplifier, and lots of compartments to store the records in. He discovered the whole thing in a German phonographic magazine which claims that you can have a live orchestra in your own front room any time you like. It's taking a long time to build and even longer for all the parts to arrive in from Sweden and Germany. The speaker frame is already finished and standing in the front room – a giant, triangular-shaped wooden box about five feet high, taking over an entire corner to itself. It's been constructed with cavity walls filled with sand to stop any distortion in the sound. He has been drying the sand out in small glass jars for weeks, placing them in the oven for an hour at a time and then pouring them into the wall around the speaker. There's even a small shutter at the bottom to let in the air.

Now he's begun to work on the cabinet itself. He's got a pencil stub balancing on the top of his ear as he explains to us how each panel has to be dovetailed and fitted together, how each compartment has to have its own door on piano hinges with its own little lock and key. All the wires connecting up the turntable and the amplifier at the back will be hidden. Very soon, the system will be up and running, and my mother says we'll be able to hear them turning the pages in the orchestra. But then he's looking at the plans again, turning the sheets upside down and wondering why one part of the unit refuses to fit. He says he should have marked every section with a little arrow or a number. My mother reads over the instructions once more and he holds pieces of wood in his hands, sticking his tongue out the side of his mouth. Everybody in the house has to be quiet and not make things worse, but then it comes, at the worst possible moment, a word in the English language, the foreign language, the forbidden language.

'Help.'

It's my sister Maria, trapped under the stairs. When

you open the in-between door in our house while somebody is in the pantry under the stairs, they won't be able
to get out. We used to take prisoners and lock each other
in. Now and again it happens to my mother and she
laughs because it's like spending time in jail with only
tins of peas and jars of jam all around you. This time it's
Maria accidentally locked in, but my father drops all the
wood and comes storming out because he thinks it's my
fault.

'What have you done?' he shouts.

'Nothing.'

The instant denial. My mother says it's always the
perpetrators who claim they were just minding their own
business. You don't deny something you didn't do. But
why should I feel guilty? I'm secretly thrilled to be
accused in the wrong and stand there smiling until my
father rushes forward to hit me on the side of my face. It
comes so fast that I lose my balance. My hand goes up to
my ear and I see the look of anger in his eyes. Sadness, too,
as if he can't help lashing out, as if it's not really him
at all, but the countless lashes he got himself that have
suddenly compelled him into this summary punishment
in the hallway. All the punishment in history passed on,
lash by lash.

'Go to your room,' he shouts.

My mother tries to stop him, but it's too late and I'm
already walking up the stairs with heavy feet, turning
around to give him a last look of poisoned glory. It's a
miscarriage of justice. You have punished the innocent.
And then to confirm it, Maria comes running up the
hallway.

'He didn't do it.'

'It's a mistake,' Franz echoes behind her.

23

'Innocent as usual,' my father mutters. He goes back to try and figure out which direction each piece of wood should be facing and now it's my turn to slam the door of my room and stand at the window with my ear boiling. I know what it's like to be guilty – it makes you helpless and sick. It's like eating something really bad, like dying slowly with your stomach turning inside out from poison. Rat powder. Blue pellets for snails and slugs. I see them out there in the garden, dragging themselves away, leaving a thick yellow trail of slime and curling up in agony.

When my father comes up to apologize, I refuse to speak to him. I don't want reconciliation. I want to hold on to my anger. My moral victory. But my mother is there pushing him into the room, forcing us to make up and shake hands. He holds my face and asks me to look him in the eyes. Then he embraces me and admits that he's made a terrible mistake. I feel like a child, with my head rammed against his chest. I can smell the sawdust in his jacket. I can hear his heart beating and I can't withhold my forgiveness any longer because he is close to tears with remorse. Then he stands back and smiles. He says he is proud of me and admires me for taking the punishment like a man, like Kevin Barry going to his execution. My mother says I'm such a brave person, like Hans and Sophie Scholl going under the guillotine for distributing leaflets against the Nazis.

And then they're gone downstairs again. I'm left alone in my room, listening to them discussing the measurements once more. Suddenly all the wooden sections fit and I can hear him hammering away with a clear conscience while I remain upstairs, staring out at the slow death in the garden. I can't stop thinking of Kevin Barry in the moment before his execution, before they bound a cloth around his eyes. I wonder what his last memory was before being shot and if he was thinking about the time when he was growing up as a boy and never even dreamed of this end to his life. And I can't help thinking about the blade slicing through Sophie Scholl's neck and how her head must have fallen forward with a heavy thump. Even if she was hooded, there must have been some reaction on her face. Was it one of defiance or did she look shocked? Did she blink, or gasp, or sneeze maybe? Was her mouth open and did she try to say something? Could she still hear her executioners talking for a moment, saying that it was all done now, filling in the documents and marking down the exact time of death? Could she hear their footsteps before the darkness closed in around her? And what were her last thoughts, of her mother and father maybe, of happy moments in Germany, of the time they went hiking together in the mountains?

And then one day the music system is finished.

There's a smell of varnish and French polish in the house for days. When the amplifier finally arrives, we stand by watching my father as he carefully takes it out of the box and fits it into its compartment perfectly. He starts connecting up the cables and there is a factory smell every time he switches it on for a test run. He keeps working till late at night and then there is a sudden blast through the speaker, like an explosion waking up the whole house, maybe even the whole street. We jump out of bed and come running out on the landing, but he's downstairs smiling and blinking like a great inventor because it's all functioning perfectly like the magazine said.

On the evening of the unveiling, my mother makes sure everything looks right. She puts an embroidered cloth on the coffee table in the front room, with drinks and small cakes. She pours glasses of cognac and you can see how proud they both are when my father unlocks the cabinet. It's such an achievement, my mother keeps saying, as we watch him putting on a record of Elisabeth Schwarzkopf. He tells us to listen out for his favourite notes on 'Panis Angelicus' by John McCormack, followed by Kevin Barry and some songs in Irish like 'An Spailpín Fánach'. Then it's back to Beethoven and Bach. And after that he has a new idea. To see how high the volume will go without any distortion in the speaker, he makes us all sit at the top of the stairs while he puts on Bruckner. We hear the crackle of the needle going down on the record. Then he comes limping up the stairs to join us, sitting in rows at the back like a concert hall, while the full orchestra begins playing in the front room with every instrument all at once.

When the concert is over, I watch him closing the cabinet and wonder where he hides the keys. He waits till everyone is out of the room before he puts them away, so it takes me weeks to find them. I keep looking everywhere, while he's out at work. I start thinking just like him and imagine where the best place would be to hide something from your own son.

Inside the big speaker, of course. In the vent at the bottom, to the left. While I'm at home on my own one day and everybody is out of the house, I go into the front room and open everything up to put on my own record, not one of the German records or any of the Irish songs, but one that I bought myself some time ago with money saved up. It's a Beatles single called 'Get back'. I prefer the flip side, though, which has John Lennon singing 'Don't let me down'. I used to play it whenever I could on the small turntable before that broke, but now I want to hear it properly, on my father's new system, as if the Beatles are in the front room with me.

I have to be very careful because even if I leave the tiniest thing out of place, he'll know that somebody has been interfering with his things. I have to become a real criminal. I have to take a photograph in my mind of everything I touch so I can put it all back exactly as before. Then I place the record on the turntable and turn up the volume. 'Don't let me down'. I play it again and again so that people can hear it all over the street and they must be thinking it's strange that my father would be at home putting a song like that on his new music cabinet during the day.

It's like blasphemy, even hearing the words in our house, saying 'you done me good'.

The song gets more perfect every time I listen to it. I sit back in the armchair and see the girl across the street leaving her house and I know that for a few moments she must be listening to the same song as me, until she walks around the corner out of sight. Music makes people look weightless. I imagine my mother and father floating around the front room like astronauts every evening while they listen to Mozart. I can see them drinking glasses of cognac without having to hold them. Family photographs of Onkel Gerd and Ta Maria lifting off the mantelpiece up into the air. Franz Kaiser and Bertha Kaiser in Kempen floating like an ascension with the market square and the church with the red roof below them. The whole family including Onkel Ted with his white collar drifting up the stairs. All kinds of vases and table lamps and pencils and books about German and Irish history flying around under the ceiling. Now it's me listening to John Lennon and it feels like the whole world has become weightless. I feel no gravity and my feet go up onto the side of the armchair. I'm drifting out the window. Floating down the street, up above the roofs of the houses and the church, looking down at the people standing at the bus stop. Up and out and down over the harbour where I can see the lads sitting on the trellis outside the shed and Dan Turley fishing. Out across the sea I go, floating away until the place I come from is only a tiny speck below me.

Afterwards I have to put everything back. I forget nothing. I lock everything up and place the keys back inside the speaker vent in exactly the same shape as I found them. Nobody would ever know, and by the time my father comes home the echo of John Lennon is long gone, remaining only in my head and keeping me afloat.

At the dinner table, my father gives me a look of deep suspicion, as if he knows I've done something. There is a frown on his forehead, but he can prove nothing. He would have to take fingerprints. I'm innocent and untouchable. He knows that I'm breaking away now but there is nothing he can do about it. He knows that I go down to the harbour every day since the summer began, speaking English like everyone else and no longer loyal to his crusade for the Irish language. He knows that I don't want to be Irish like him, that I don't want to look like him or even listen to the same music or read the same books. I look back across the table at him, speaking English in my own head, repeating the forbidden words 'she done me good'.

And then I remember something that brings me back down to the ground again. I realize that while I was paying attention to every detail, scrupulously putting everything back in its place, I must have forgotten the most important thing of all. I left John Lennon on the turntable.

Now there's going to be trouble. I can feel the weight of my arms on the table. I'm such a bad criminal. I go back over everything step by step. I know I turned the speed from forty-five back to thirty-three. I know I locked each and every one of the compartments. I did everything right, down to the last precise detail, but I was concentrating so much on replacing everything that I forgot the most obvious thing. When my father goes to play music after dinner, he'll find a strange disc on the turntable that he would never in a million years allow into the house.

I stand up from the table in a panic. The chair makes a yelp behind me and I rush around past my mother to get to the door. Everybody looks up thinking I'm going to be sick. They stop eating to see me running past, trying to get away as fast as possible. I want to rescue John Lennon. I want to run to the front room, take out the keys quickly and remove him from the turntable before it's too late. But then I stop at the door and look back at them all sitting around the table as if they have become frozen in time. My brother Franz has a piece of carrot stuck on his fork which has stopped halfway up to his mouth. My mother has a jug in her hand but the milk has stopped pouring. My sisters are all shocked with their eyes wide open and Ita's mouth is full of mashed potato as if she's blowing up a balloon. My father is getting ready to follow me. He puts his knife and fork down with a clack. His backside is raised up from the chair, in mid-air.

It's a race against time. I know it's futile because he's bound to get there before I'm halfway through. No matter how fast I am, he will surely catch me putting away the keys or coming out with my hands behind my back and the disc under my jumper. It's no good and I turn back. I walk all the way around the table to sit down again and now they're all wondering why I'm suddenly not in a rush any more. I want to explain that I thought I needed to go to the bathroom and it's no longer that urgent. But I say nothing. My face has gone red and I feel heavy in my legs. I try to think up other schemes to get out of this. I imagine it's not happening and that John Lennon will miraculously turn into John McCormack at the last minute, but it's all hopeless.

Four

At the harbour, everybody has a new identity. It's the way my friend Packer talks about the place and about the people and about all the things that go on there, the way that he gives everybody a new role, a new life, even sometimes a new name. He has a way of persuading people to do things they never dreamed of. He can make everyone laugh and hold them up with stories. He looks into everyone's eyes and makes them believe what he's saying, even as he invents the world around him and turns the most boring day into a big legend, smiling and getting people to agree with his ideas, no matter how mad his latest plans are. When Packer is around, you step outside your own life as if you're watching yourself in a film, or reading about yourself in a book. He has a gift for making everybody feel like they have been newly invented and that the harbour is a fictional place, out of this world, on a big screen in front of us.

We sit outside the shed listening to Packer talking about Dan Turley, while he's out in the boat, pulling up the lobster pots. Packer describes all the things nobody even notices about themselves. He talks about how Dan pays us at the end of the week, calling each one of us into the shed individually while the others are not watching, how he pulls a few notes out of his pocket and hands them over secretly with his hand down-turned and shaking a little, as if you're the only one getting paid. He tells us how Dan gives away nothing about his life, how he trusts nobody and thinks the whole world is a conspiracy against him. Even the sea and the tides are trying to trick Dan Turley. In a low voice, Packer tells us how Dan has enemies at the harbour, how his shed was burned down once and nobody ever found out who did it. Something big is going to happen at the harbour very soon, Packer assures us, and you don't want to be absent when it does. He says Dan Turley never smiles and often stares at the sea with his eyes narrowed, as if he has a fair idea who burned down his shed, and even though he can do nothing about it yet, he's just patiently biding his time.

Even when Dan comes back in with the lobster and stands leaning in the doorway of the shed again, Packer still talks about him as if he's a made-up character. Right in front of him, he begins to imitate the way Dan talks out the side of his mouth all the time, cursing through his teeth. 'Hooken hell' or 'hooken clown', he mutters, because it's a public place and Dan can't be offending the decent people passing by. Packer repeats the way he gives orders, the way he shouts when he's pissed off with you for making mistakes and bringing the boat around on the wrong side. 'Tha' other side,' Packer says, because that's how Dan pronounces it in his Northern accent, leaving long spaces between the words as if he is exhausted and this is the last time he wants to say these words.

'Tha' – other – side.'

The harbour lads all start repeating the words until Dan goes inside and comes back out with a big hatchet he keeps for self-defence ever since the shed was burned down. Everybody suddenly runs away even though Dan is only joking and wouldn't really use the hatchet on us, because we're on his side. Packer is the only person who can put his arm around Dan and get him to put away the hatchet. 'Tha' hooken other side...' everyone keeps saying to each other all the time, because it's become a big joke by now and Dan has to listen to himself echoing all over the bay. But you don't make fun of Dan for long. You know when he's serious, because he doesn't need a hatchet to prove it, and Packer tells us about the time he chased these young people all the way up the hill to the Shangri La Hotel one day and dragged them back down to the harbour to pay for their boat trip, even though he's over seventy. Nobody messes with Dan Turley.

When all the lads on motorbikes arrive down on the pier with girls on the back, it looks like they have been invented by Packer. They arrive with lots of noise and smoke and park in a line until Dan starts muttering about them blocking up the whole pier. We stare at the bikes and at the girls, one of them looking at herself in the wing mirror and kissing her own lips. Somebody asks Dan to turn up the radio, but he ignores it and disappears inside the shed, waiting for the weather forecast. Somebody starts fidgeting with one of the motorbikes, turning the throttle or testing the brakes, until the owner tells him to get his filthy, fucking, mackerel-stinking hands off.

Then the harbour lads are laughing again, saying: 'Hookin' hell, can you not leave the thing alone? Go on, smash it, why don't yee?' The owner of the motorbike then has to pull his jumper down over his hand and clean the mackerel scales off the chrome handlebars. Packer tells the story about how one of the motorbike lads called 'Whiskey' ran out of juice one day and just robbed a bottle of Jameson off his father, enough to get him as

33

far as the garage to fill up again. They laugh and argue. 'Hooken dreaming,' they say. They could easily disprove the story and say that whiskey would ruin the engine, but it's like everything else at the harbour, they want to enter into the legend that Packer invents around us. They believe his story and even pass it on themselves later. And all the time, Packer has his own words and phrases for describing people, like 'vulgar' and 'venomous' and 'vile and ordinary'. He has the harbour lads going around calling each other 'shrunken paps' and 'mackerel mickies', using an invented vocabulary that nobody else under-stands but us.

'Hark, you shrunken mackerel mickies.'

Packer has given me a new identity as well. He describes me as the silent observer and makes it sound like a great talent to speak only when you need to. I don't have a story for myself, so Packer makes one up for me and even gives me a new name, 'Vlad the Inhaler', because of my lungs. Everybody knows that I've got trouble breathing and that I still have the dogs howling in my chest some-times. Packer has noticed that when somebody asks me a question, I take in a deep breath before answering. He says I breathe as if I'm still discovering how to do it, like figuring out the gears on a motorbike. He says I'm still counting in and out as if I'm never going to get enough air and that the air doesn't really belong to me. I'm only borrowing the air around me instead of really owning it like everyone else. So now he's given me a new name and a new identity and I go home covered in mackerel scales every day. There's always a smell of petrol on my hands from handling the engines and also these dried-out mackerel scales all over everything I touch. Tiny silver coins on my fingernails, on my shoes, even on the books

I read at home. I feel I've turned into a mackerel myself, breathing underwater and shedding flaky scales everywhere I go, travelling at thirty miles an hour as if I'm on the run and cannot stand still.

Then one day, when Packer went off on the back of a motorbike, I went back to myself again. Out of nowhere I saw my mother walking down along the road by the castle and the nursing home with my little brother Ciarán on his bike. At first, I thought there was something wrong and she needed to tell me something that happened. But then I realized that she only wanted to see where I worked, because I was always coming home with mackerel and stories about being out in boats, trying to describe my life the way Packer does, speaking like him about all the funny things going on at the harbour. But that didn't mean I wanted anyone from my house to follow me down there. It was my place. It was where I got away from my family. And now my mother was coming. I saw them turning on to the pier, with my little brother just ahead on his bike, stopping every few minutes to let her catch up.

I could not allow this to happen. They would blow my cover. Any minute now, everybody at the harbour would find out that I was German, so I slipped away, up around the rocks at the back of the shed. Nobody noticed me leaving. I hid in a place where I could still see what was going on at the pier, hoping my mother would just go away again.

Dan must have thought she had come to buy some fish, but then I saw her talking to him and even shaking hands with him, looking into the shed to see if it really was the way I had described it to her, with all the engines in a row and the yellow life jackets hanging up like invisible people standing around the walls. I saw Dan bending down and asking Ciarán to show him the home-made gun he was carrying with him. It was a gun he made without any help from anyone, out of wood and all kinds of metal parts that he collected together. We were never allowed to buy guns in our house, so Ciarán made his own with a bathroom lock as a bolt and gun-sights made from Meccano parts. My father once told him that nobody was allowed to bring guns to the table in times of peace, but my mother said it was a special home-made gun that came from his own imagination. It was called a peacemaker, so he was always allowed to hang it around the back of the chair.

Dan only knows my first name, so maybe he didn't make any connection between me and my mother. It was possible that he thought she was a tourist. He was pointing at the boats and pointing inside the shed. I was still hoping that she would just disappear again, but then I saw Dan pointing up towards the rocks. I hid down as low as I could, without falling off into the water. Then I heard my mother at the foot of the rocks calling me. My little brother Ciarán as well, both of them echoing each other from different places.

'Hanni,' they were calling, her nickname for me, 'Hanni.'

I could not move. I was like a dead fish, covered in mackerel scales, unable to breathe. I didn't want to do this thing of not answering her, but I had to. I felt sorry for my mother because she had no friends in Ireland except her own children. I didn't want to deny her like this, but I could not let anyone know that I had a German mother, so I made her disappear out of my mind, out of my life completely. The language she was using was not my language. I un-remembered my whole family and all my brothers and sisters. I un-remembered all the stories she told me and all the cakes she baked, even the way she folded clothes. I denied that I had ever seen the photographs of where she grew up. I denied that I had ever been to Kempen on holidays. I un-remembered all the people I had met, all my aunts and uncles, all the parcels that came over at Christmas with sweets and chocolates, all the story books and all the clothes. I denied everything I grew up with and made the country that my mother came from disappear off the map.

'Hanni,' I heard Ciarán calling.

He was shooting the seagulls. I could hear myself breathing hard and there was nobody I wanted to talk to more than my mother.

'Come on, let's go,' I heard her say.

I watched them leaving again with Ciarán cycling ahead, both of them stopping now and again to look back. I waited until they went out of sight at the nursing home, before I came out again.

Later on that same day, a schoolteacher from the convent school up the road came down to the harbour. I had seen her many times before, going up on the rocks to sunbathe. This time she drove right up the pier and got out of the car, dressed up with a pearl necklace and light green scarf across her shoulders. She came over to the shed to ask if we had any lobster. It was left to me to get the weighing scales. She followed me over to the side of the pier and I could hear her shoes clicking after me. She stood right behind me as I pulled up the lobster storage box, scraping against the harbour wall as it came up, water gushing out through the sides.

When the box was on the pier, I undid the rope that

kept the lid down and started taking out the lobster one by one, so she could take a look at them. I could smell her perfume in the air all around me. Her dress was flapping with the breeze coming in from the sea and she had to hold it down. I thought she would recognize who I was, so I spoke without looking at her very much. There were about a dozen lobster in the box, all with their claws tied with black rubber bands to stop them fighting each other and to make it easy to pick them out. When she kneeled down to look into the box for herself, I could see right down into her dress and had to look away again.

After I weighed various lobster, she decided on two of them which I set aside for her. I closed the box, calculated the price and she got out her purse from a velvet green bag. But as she was handing me the money, she looked right into my face and smiled.

'You're the German boy, aren't you?' she said.

I shook my head and looked at the ground.

'Yes you are. Your mother is that lovely German woman who bakes cakes for the school?' she said, but I kept shaking my head.

'No. Not me.'

I knew she didn't believe me, because she kept on looking into my eyes to see if she could get the truth out of me. I stared down at the lobster on the pier trying to open their claws and crawl away. She gave me the money and I put the lobster into a plastic bag for her. She said thanks and waited for a moment to see if I still might admit that I was German, but then she finally walked away across the pier. I saw the harbour boys all staring at her getting back into her car, holding her dress down to make sure the wind didn't blow it up and show her legs.

I tied up the box and dropped it back down over the

edge of the pier, scraping the wall as it descended. About halfway down, I saw the lid coming loose again. I hadn't tied it well enough and now it was opening up. I looked around and saw everybody still watching the school-teacher driving away. I tried to pull the box back up again, but that made everything worse. The lid flew open and the lobster started falling out, into the water below. There was nothing I could do. I pulled it right up onto the pier, but the remaining lobster were gone. I thought of jumping off the pier, diving down to search for them underwater. I thought of going over to Dan and telling him what had happened, offering to pay for them myself. But I wasn't strong enough to do that. I had the weakness and I could think of nothing else but tying the lid down properly this time and letting the box down again into the water, hoping that nobody would think it was my fault.

When I got home, the house was silent and deserted, as if everybody had gone away. I walked in the door to find the oak trunk open. My mother had let history out again. It was all over the house and I could feel it in the air, like a special stillness in the rooms. There was no sound except the clocks ticking backwards. The door into the front room was open, holding its breath. The furniture seemed shocked and motionless, as if nothing would move on until the oak trunk was closed again. This is the ancient German trunk that came over to Dublin from her home in Kempen after the war. It's where she keeps all her things and I could smell the candles and the Christmas decorations, the old letters and documents, even the smell of pine needles. It's where she keeps her diaries, her old passports, all her precious possessions.

I searched through the rooms until I found my mother

upstairs, sitting on her bed, leafing through the small leather-bound book that she carried in her suitcase from Germany when she first arrived in Ireland. She didn't notice me coming in, as if she was completely in her own world, even though my brothers and sisters were in the room as well. We watched her putting the ancient book up to her face and inhaling the smell of the old pages, trying to go back to the time of Gutenberg when the book was printed. She glanced over the old lettering and stopped to admire the beginning of each chapter, where the first letter is spread over the entire page and coloured in with an intricate design, like a small German version of the Book of Kells. She was given this book as a gift by the family of her best friend in Mainz for helping them with food when people in Germany had nothing. It's one of the few treasures she has, one that she takes out whenever she's homesick and wants to remember where she comes from.

But this time it was more than that. I asked her what was wrong, but she remained silent. I thought it had something to do with me denying her at the harbour and that she would not speak to me any more. Beside her on the bed, there was a letter, left open with the envelope next to it. It had a German stamp and I knew she must have read the letter many times over already. Ciarán was playing with his cars on the floor of the room, making buzzing noises. And then my mother spoke as if she was talking to herself.

'I don't understand it,' she said at last.

'What?'

'The book. They want it back.'

They were asking if she was still holding on to it for them. For safe-keeping, it said in the letter. She held the book close to her chest as if she expected them to come walking in the door any minute to take it away from her. It was like owning something precious that belonged to a museum. They had given it to her after the war when it was worth nothing, when the family wanted to show how grateful they were for all that she had done for them, keeping them alive with food. But now it had become valuable and there was a question of ownership. My mother never spoke of it being valuable. She loved it only because it was such a beautiful gift that was hundreds of years old and given to her under extraordinary circumstances.

'Does it mean nothing to them any more?' she asked.

I told her to write back and say she hasn't got it. Say you've lost it, I suggested. Say you don't know what they're talking about. What old book printed around the time of Gutenberg about the lives of saints? My mother looked at me as if I was trying to persuade her to commit a crime. She could not lie. She would have to write back, tell them that it was the most treasured thing in the house apart from her own children. How could they think of asking her to give it back? She looked at the letter once more and said they had made her feel like a thief, as if she had taken it off them at a bad time, a time of crisis. That she was withholding it from its rightful owner. She felt that what she did in Mainz was no longer worth anything and that the memory of it has become undone by time. That everything was being taken back now and she was losing not just the book but one of her most precious memories as well.

'Stefan is coming over to visit us,' she said. 'We better get ready.'

Stefan is the son of my mother's school friend, Tante

Käthe. I remember going to stay with them in Mainz when we were small. I remember Onkel Ulrich and Tante Käthe's chemist shops in the city. Onkel Ulrich has a straight leg from the time that he was injured in the war. I saw him at Mass, keeping his right leg straight out and nobody making much of a fuss about it except us. I remember trying it out for myself for days, imagining what it would be like to be shot and not being able to bend one knee as long as you live. And Stefan. I remember Stefan because he was a good bit older than me and he didn't really want to have much to do with us or let us play with his toys. And now he was grown up and coming over to Ireland to collect the book which they had given to my mother as a gift. Maria told my mother she should hide it in the attic. Ita said it was against the law to take back a gift. My mother put her arms around them and said she would never give the book back, no more than she would ever give away one of her own children.

That night I could hear her downstairs discussing it all with my father and him saying they had no moral right to demand back a gift that was given in good faith. Even when we were all in bed and the whole house was silent, everybody was still thinking about the book and where it should be hidden. I was thinking about Germany after the war and all the bombed-out cities. I thought of Stefan coming over and taking away the book from my mother and her crying because the last bit of Germany was going to be gone now. I thought about the lobster underwater, helplessly crawling through the seaweed with black rubber bands tied around their claws. I thought about how I betrayed my mother and how the lobster were making their way back out along the seabed, lost and defenceless, unable to open up their claws.

Five

It started long before that, one year around Halloween
when we tried to make friends with everybody. Myself and
my brother Franz wanted to stop being outsiders, on our
own all the time. We wanted to be insiders from now on,
like everyone else in Ireland, so we decided to try and find
some way of getting in with them. I started practising
English on my own, saying things to the wall like 'What
are you lookin' at?' I rehearsed conversations out loud in
my room, threatening to kick the shit out of the wardrobe
and telling the door to watch out or else I would go over
and straighten his face for him. I even practised the walk
that they had around our place that my mother calls the
'Glasthule Swagger'. I stopped to glance sideways at
myself in the mirror before going out. I was the hard man
of the house and I felt as real as anyone else out there.

They were collecting wood for weeks. I watched them
after school carrying pallets and broken planks through
the streets, all working together. Some of them had super-
market trolleys stacked up with junk from building sites,
sheets of timber with rusty nails sticking out, anything
that would burn. It's the same every year. They keep it all
hidden until the night of Halloween. Everybody knows
where the bonfire is going to be, in the park with the railings, with the red-bricked national school on one side

and the terraces of red-bricked corporation houses on the other. Every year, they say it's going to be bigger than ever before. And every year, by the time the flames reach the height of the houses and the sparks begin to drift across the roofs, somebody calls the fire brigade and there's trouble.

We wanted to be part of the big fire, so we found a wooden door in the laneway and decided to carry it down on the afternoon of Halloween. The blue paint was peeling off and it was submerged in weeds, but we kicked away the nettles and carried it down the street with the snails and worms still clinging on to one side. It was so heavy that we had to put it down every now and again along the way. Franz had the idea that we should roll it down on an old axle and wheels that we had from an old pram, but we were already halfway and just carried on. By the time we got there, they had begun to pile up the wood for the fire, so we brought it straight in through the gates of the park. We didn't talk or say anything. We thought it was a good time for a truce, with everybody on the same side, so we placed our door standing up along with all their wood.

'Look, it's the Nazis,' one of them said.

I was afraid they would tell us to fuck off and take away our door. But they needed every piece of wood they could get. They didn't care if it was Nazi wood.

'It's a German door,' they said. 'It'll burn like fuck.'

It felt strange to be helping the people who have always been against us, as if we were betraying ourselves. But it felt good at the same time because we were all going to be friends now for the sake of the fire. My mother says you have to be careful because they are the fist people and they never change. I knew they still wanted to put us on trial

44

for being German. They still wanted to execute us, but maybe the night of the bonfire was the big moment where we could all forget history, I thought. Maybe they would overlook all that and allow us to take part.

We stood back to watch. There were two of them standing on top, pulling a broken bedside locker up on a rope. Everybody shouting and helping, passing in planks of wood through the railings and throwing car tyres around the base. A small boy brought a pile of ice-pop sticks. As it started getting dark, nobody paid much attention to us any more and we looked as Irish as everyone else.

At dinner, my mother helped us to escape. She doesn't like fire. She's afraid of things burning and the smell of smoke reminds her of the war, but she explained to my father that we had to be there because our contribution was made and we had to see our door in flames. It was fully dark outside now and I could hear bangers going off. My father looked angry, but I knew he was happy underneath because Halloween was an ancient Irish invention which they had in West Cork as well and the word bonfire in English came from the Irish words 'Tinte Cnáimh', the fires of bones. The day of the dead. As long as we didn't speak English or take any of his wood, he said he had nothing against us going, so we ran down to see them starting the fire. I even had three bangers which I bought in the city from a woman on Moore Street who kept them under her apron. We let them off and our bangs were adding to all the other noise of rockets lighting up the sky around us.

There were children everywhere going around with masks and plastic bags full of treats. We used to do that as well, but everybody knew who we were underneath, because my mother always made the masks herself and they looked like German wolves and German monsters. The streets were full of gangs of children dressed up as Frankenstein. Sometimes there were three Draculas in one group, all looking the same but in different heights and ages. There were older people as well, on their way to a Halloween party somewhere. A girl dressed as an angel, in a miniskirt and high, black shiny boots and wings on her back, accompanied by a doctor in a white coat swinging a stethoscope around in his hand and chasing children away who were asking for cigarettes. There was fog and smoke everywhere, even before they started the fire the air was heavy and damp, like cold steam.

At the park, they were all gathering to watch one of the older boys on top of the wooden structure with a canister, pouring petrol over the top. Another boy poured petrol all around the sides. Finally, a cheer echoed around the terraces and the yellow light of the flames was reflected on the walls and in the windows and in the faces all around the fire. Even the railings turned gold.

It didn't take long for the sparks to crack. There was shouting and somebody called it an inferno. They were shielding their eyes from the flames with their elbows. Others were drinking beer and smoking as they threw bits of lighting wood that had fallen out, back in again. Our blue door was in flames now and it looked as if you could open it and walk straight into the interior of the fire. It was the door to hell. My brother Franz and I stood watching like everyone else. We were the inferno-brothers. We had dark eyes and yellow faces, as if we had just come back out from inside the fire and shut the flaming door behind us.

And then we could hear the fire-brigade siren in the

distance. The sparks were being carried across the roof of the school and we knew what was coming. As soon as the blue light of the fire brigade began to flash around the terraces, Franz moved back.

'I'm going now,' he said.

I tried to make him stay but he didn't want trouble. He doesn't want to witness anything like my mother witnessed in Germany. I told him not to be so scared of things, but he was suddenly gone from my side. And maybe it's easier when I'm on my own, to feel that I belong to them now.

As soon as the fire brigade pulled up outside the railings, the jeers began from inside. Cursing and booing. Somebody said it was a riot, but the firemen ignored it all and smiled. It wasn't so long ago that they were doing this kind of thing themselves, but now it was their duty to put it out. They un-spooled the hose and directed the water at the flames. As the fire began to hiss, the boys started throwing things, empty beer cans and loose branches. Then it was sods of grass which they picked up all around them in the park, harmlessly hitting the black uniforms of the firemen as if they didn't even notice.

I belonged to the Irish fire now. I was carried away by the anger of the crowd and had no option but to pick up a sod of my own, not so much to hit anyone but to prove that the fire mattered as much to me as it did to them. The firemen were reducing the great flames to nothing. You could feel the heat fading and the shouts becoming more hostile. Bastards. Fuckers. I heard myself joining in. Words I had only heard them use against me, now became my words too.

More sods were thrown. Bigger ones. This time I picked up the heaviest sod I could find. I pulled at the long grass until a large clump of earth came loose and it felt like I was holding a severed head by the hair. I could hardly swing it around me. The trouble was that when I let go, I discovered my aim was a lot better than I imagined. I could already see that it was going to hit one of the firemen directly in the head. It flew through the yellow air like a black skull with grassy golden hair flying back. I could see the shock in his eyes as the sod crashed into the side of his face, just as he turned his head around.

'You little bastard,' he shouted.

He wiped his eyes and brushed bits of soil out of his collar, then straightened his helmet.

'Sorry, mister,' I said.

I wanted to tell him I didn't actually mean to hit him. But it was already too late for that because the boys around me were cheering.

'Great shot.'

'Look, he knocked the fuckin' head off a fireman.'

For the first time ever, I had done something which made me into a hero. I would be accepted now. They were saying the Germans were amazing marksmen to be able to hit somebody from that distance with a sod. Every time I would walk down the street from now on, they would think of me as the guy who clobbered the fireman. I would no longer be an outsider and they would be clapping me on the back, asking me to do it again, to see if I could break a street light with a stone. But as they kept cheering and laughing, I knew they were making things worse for me, because now I had the fireman to deal with.

'Sorry,' I said once more. 'I didn't mean it.'

I saw the rage in the fireman's face and ran away, hoping that he wouldn't follow me. I heard the sound of him cursing and his heavy boots thudding in the grass behind me. There was no escape. I was going to arrive at the railings and be trapped, away from the fire and away from the crowd, with nobody coming to stand by me.

At the corner, I turned around to beg for mercy with my hands up. There was a gap in the railings, but I didn't really believe I could get away. I knew there were bars missing in other places, where boys crossed the park rather than walking all the way around. I was too numb to think of escaping, so got ready to surrender.

'Please mister, don't hit me,' I said. 'It was an accident.'

The fireman slowed down to a walk because he knew he had me cornered. Even in the darkness I could see from his eyes that he was not going to show me any mercy. At that last minute, I decided to try and climb through the bars. I felt his hand on my neck and heard his voice saying 'little fucker' in my ear. He was too big to get through the gap himself, but his arm was stretched out through the bars holding on firmly to my clothes.

'Stop him,' he shouted at some men walking by on their way to Eagle House for a drink. He tried to drag me back in through the gap and I was pulling away with my foot up against the railings.

'Hold the little bastard for me.'

Some of the boys came up to see what was happening. They had lost interest in the fire which was almost gone out by now.

'Look, it's Eichmann,' one of them said.

They had turned against me. They no longer saw me as a hero who had done something to defend the big fire. It was a mistake to have even tried getting in with them, because they were on the side of the fireman now, staring at me through the bars, waiting to see what would happen. All I could think of doing was to chop at the fireman's hand and release myself from his grip.

'Get him,' the fireman shouted, and some of the men outside the railings began to converge on me. One of them with a red face threw down his cigarette and stepped into my way. I dodged him, but he came after me until he started coughing and stood still. I felt their hands on me, but I managed to twist and pull away from them each time, even when they put a foot out to trip me. Another man came after me, but the change in his pockets started falling out and rolling towards the gutter, with him cursing and calling me a whore and bending down to pick up his money.

I was afraid to run further into the terraces. I tried to turn back, but some of the boys had begun to come through the gap in the fence.

'It's Eichmann,' they were shouting. 'After him.'

I was running down their streets. Rockets were going off all around me. Children staring at me through their masks. Women standing outside their houses smoking and talking, watching me running past with my shirt and my jumper torn. Some of the doors were wide open and you could see right into the front rooms where the television was on. I thought the women were going to get out the dustbin lids and start banging. One of the women was laughing or coughing, I didn't know which, and a terrier dog ran out barking and chasing after me because he knew I didn't belong to that street.

Then I remembered how this happened to my mother, a long time ago, when she was small. She told me how the Kaiser girls played on the Buttermarkt Square in Kempen, right in front of their house, and sometimes they clogged up the fountain with paper from their father's stationery shop and the water swept all across the square and the town warden complained to their father. The town warden even chased them into the house one day. But instead of protecting them, their grandmother let him right into the house to teach them a lesson that would put an end to the complaints. My mother was the only one who ran out the back door and into the streets again, while the other girls were all caught in the hallway by the warden and their grandmother, facing punishment. My mother ran through the streets of the town all afternoon, around by the Burg, by the windmill, running and running, thinking that the warden was after her all the time. Even when it got dark she was still afraid to go home. But then she was even more afraid of being left out all night, so she decided to give herself up. When she got home at last, sneaking up silently to her own house, the warden was gone, but she had to explain to her father why she had come home so late after everyone had eaten their dinner and the table was already cleared. So then she told him about the town warden chasing them into the house and how she was the only one who wasn't caught. She expected her father to be angry, but he smiled. He put her on his knee and stroked her head until she was not so afraid any more.

Now it's me running away, just like my mother. Now it's the fireman and all the other bonfire boys coming after me through the streets. The fireman must have got out through the park gate because I saw him following me all the way with the boys ahead of him, running hard and catching up fast. Further back, some of the men were following, too, and I was afraid the whole city was after me. I was afraid the women would try to bar my way and that nobody would tell the fireman to have mercy on me.

At the end of the street I didn't know which way to

turn, so I climbed up onto the roof of a parked car and from there onto a wall that had some glass shards sticking out of the top. I could see nothing below me on the far side. I couldn't even see how deep it was. It was black down there and no matter how much I stared down, waiting for my eyes to get used to the dark, I was blind and afraid to jump. I held my hands out in front of me as if that would help me find out what was down there on the other side, desperately searching for a safe place to land. I had no idea what I was going to jump into and thought I would be impaled on spikes. I thought of vicious dogs. I thought my chin would hit a tree stump or an upturned wheelbarrow. I thought maybe there was nothing down there at all and that I would just keep falling without ever reaching the ground.

I waited on the top of the wall until they caught up with me and I could see them below on the pavement. Some of them were already getting up on the car. The fireman was reaching his arm up along the wall to try and drag me back down again. So I jumped into the unknown. I threw myself into the darkness and kept falling down, down, for ever into the dark until I disappeared.

Six

After that I was afraid the fireman would turn up at the door of our house. If he couldn't punish me himself, then he would try and get my father to punish me instead. I couldn't sleep because I thought they would come and arrest me as a juvenile offender. I tried to work out what I would say, how I would lie to them and say it was dark and the fireman got it all wrong. It wasn't me. They would call me a delinquent and ask me why I ran away if I was so innocent. The fireman would bring witnesses who would point at me and say: that's him, Eichmann. But I would stare them all out and say it was a mistaken identity. Only my mother would be on my side and believe me.

Nobody came to the house. But that didn't mean it was all forgotten. I knew they were still after me, so I had to go on the run, like Eichmann in Argentina. From then on, I had to avoid being seen on the streets. I had to become invisible and find ways of getting around without anyone noticing me. I drew up a map of detours through laneways and gardens. Instead of walking straight down to the seafront along the street, I started going around by the edge of the football field, across the disused farm, through the timber yard. I invented all kinds of complex escape routes around the neighbourhood, through building sites and derelict land. I got to know every foothold in the wall and every gap in the barbed wire.

I decided that I had to go underground. I had to pretend I didn't exist any more. Nobody saw me going to school on the train in the morning. Nobody saw me coming home. Of course there was always a chance they might be waiting for me on one of my secret routes, that I would be trapped and put on trial again. Franz always thought it was safer to be out in the open where there were more adults around. But I trained myself to stay out of sight. Occasionally, somebody would spot me crawling for a few feet along the top of a wall. I would hear a shout or an angry knock on the window behind me, but I was always long gone before anyone took much notice. I would see people in their houses, in the kitchen with the lights on, sitting at the table with their backs to the window having their tea, people watching TV with blue faces, and me passing by outside like a gust of wind. I was living underwater now, running along the sea floor and breathing in silence.

Even at home, I became invisible. My mother said we'd always been doing strange and unusual things like putting stones in our ears when we were small, but this was one of the oddest things she had ever heard of and she hoped I wasn't starting to lose my mind. She said I was going around the place like a ghost and one evening, when she called me to dinner, I didn't go down the stairs but out through the window instead. I stepped past the beehives, climbed down onto the garden wall and came in through the back door. Then I sat down at the table without a word, as if I was totally out of sight. She even played along with it for a while, asking if anyone had seen me. But then she begged me to come back to life again because she was worried that I might disappear into myself. She waved her hand in front of my eyes and made faces at me until I had to laugh.

'You can't go underground in your own home,' she said.

At the dinner table, I started speaking to myself in English. Every evening I looked at my father in front of me and I was having a big conversation inside my own head in the forbidden language. He must have known that I was breaking his rules, but there was nothing he could do to stop me speaking to myself in secret as if I had disappeared to a different country.

My mother said she understood why you sometimes have to become invisible. She remembers the time under the Nazis when Onkel Gerd, the Lord Mayor, had to disappear because he was silenced and they threw him out of office for not agreeing to join the party. First it was people like Onkel Gerd who were invisible, she says, but then it was the Jews who could not be seen anywhere on the streets in Germany. My father says the Irish also went underground against the British. He says they lost their language and now they're all walking around like ghosts, following maps with invisible streets and invisible place names. He says the Irish are still in hiding in a foreign language. But one of these days they'll come out and speak their own language again.

At night I stayed awake, thinking of more and more ways of getting around without being seen by anyone, imagining tunnels where I could actually move from place to place under the streets and come up through manholes. I imagined that I could vanish and live without ever touching the streets, without breathing. I imagined that if they ever caught me, I would vanish into thin air right in front of their eyes. I imagined clever things to say in English that would distract them and give me a chance to escape again. I thought about how I jumped off the wall into the darkness. I lay in bed and kept falling for ever. I thought my mother was falling as well. All my aunts and uncles in Germany falling down without ever reaching the ground, everybody in Germany just going down, down, down, without stopping. Until I started getting headaches all the time and I was no longer able to get up and go to school. All the invisible maps of the world were no good to me and the headaches got so bad that I just wished I could give myself up and get it over with.

When Eichmann was discovered living underground in Argentina, they were able to identify him by the injuries to his head which he suffered once in a motorbike accident, before he joined the SS. After being in hiding for so long, he was lonely and felt that anything was better than being invisible. When they walked up to him at a bus stop and identified him as Adolf Eichmann, the man who organized the transport of Jewish people to the concentration camps, he was probably shocked at first because it sounded like the worst insult in the world, the curse of his own name coming after him all these years later. He must have thought of denying it, but there was no point. Perhaps he was relieved to be himself again. He didn't want to be imprisoned or executed, but he didn't want the pain of being invisible either. People say that he was given a choice right there and then at the bus stop, whether he would prefer to be executed on the spot or travel to Jerusalem to be put on trial. So he agreed to go on trial because he wanted recognition. He was fed up being a nobody in Argentina. He didn't own up to his guilt or ever say that he was remorseful. He didn't admit to his crimes and said he was only doing his duty, trying to be as efficient as possible. He wanted to be famous for doing a great job, better than anyone else in the world had ever done before that. He wanted to stay alive for ever in history.

This time the doctors knew exactly what was wrong with me and called it Meningitis. I walked to the ambulance with a red blanket around my shoulders. My mother stood at the gate with her hand over her mouth, crying. She couldn't come in the ambulance with me because she had to stay at home and look after the others. The neighbours were out as well and they were all worried because I was going to a place called Cherry Orchard and not everybody came back.

When I arrived at the hospital, there was no urgency at all at first. I had to lie in bed and wait, watching the man beside me smoking cigarettes and making a leather purse. He had a small radio on the locker beside his bed with lots of songs like 'Going on a summer holiday' coming back on again and again as if no time was going by at all. After about ten or fifteen summer holidays they brought me into the theatre and put me face-down on the operating table.

There were three of them holding me down and one of the nurses explained that Meningitis was a killer disease. They would have to stick a needle into my back in order to take some fluid from my spine. It had to be done without any anaesthetic, she explained, so they held my arms and legs and my head down, and I felt the needle going right into my back like a knife.

As soon as it touched my spine, I screamed. I screamed so much that they had to stop. I could be heard all over the hospital, but I didn't care because the needle was so painful that I couldn't help screaming each time, until they stopped. They were unable to find any fluid in my spine at first, so they had to keep trying in different places, until I was nearly fainting and the surgeon finally took off his mask because he was getting angry.

'Do you think I'm trying to torture you?' he said.

'Please,' I said. 'It's a mistake. I jumped down off the wall.'

I tried to explain that I must have banged my head and that's why I was getting the headaches. It wasn't Meningitis.

'What's he babbling about?' the surgeon asked.

The nurses shook their heads. They must have thought I was getting delirious from Meningitis and that I no longer knew what I was saying. I tried to get off the operating table and had one leg hanging down with my foot nearly touching the floor, trying to escape. But they kept pushing me back up and finally they pinned every arm and leg down again.

'Are we ready?' the surgeon said.

This time they didn't care what language I screamed in. One of the nurses said it would be over soon, but it went on for ever. They put the needle in again and again, until I was hoarse from crying. Eventually I felt their hands go soft and I knew they were letting me go. I heard the nurse saying that I was a free man. They brought me back to the ward and there was a piece of cake left on the bed along with a note from my mother, saying she was sorry that she missed me.

Then I was back watching the man smoking in his bed and not saying much, listening to more summer holidays for hours and hours, waiting for the results. They didn't find any Meningitis and I was afraid they would have to do more tests. When my mother came to visit me again the next time, she stayed sitting on my bed for as long as she could. I begged her not to go and she stayed until the very last minute, until well after the bell rang and all the other visitors were gone.

'*Mein Schatz*,' she said. 'You'll be home soon.'

They found no evidence of Meningitis. It was like being declared innocent and my father came to collect me. He brought a bag with my clothes and it felt strange to be wearing shoes again. He was smiling a lot and speaking to me in Irish, saying I would notice a few changes in the house. I was like an emigrant returning home, dying to see if anything was still the same.

Everything was different. The house looked smaller than it did before. The street we live on seemed to have moved a bit further in from the sea and our back garden looked like it was squashed. The grass had grown. There were leaves on all the trees. My mother was wearing her navy blue dress with a white collar and I was like a visitor who had never been to our house before. Bríd and Ita were dressed up as nurses. Maria showed me the new washing machine, and the new green paint on the back door. Franz said the bees had swarmed while I was in hospital and nobody was at home to catch them or bring them back, so they got away. He said he came home from school one day and saw a big cloud of bees moving out over the gardens and over the roofs of the houses, so he ran up the road after them to see where they were going, until they went out of sight over the chestnut trees, across the railway tracks, and he couldn't keep up with them any more. At dinner, Ciarán wanted to sit next to me. Everybody was looking at me and I was glad we were all in the same country again.

When the time came to execute Eichmann, they had to discuss what to do with his body afterwards. The court decided that he should be executed by hanging, but there were no instructions given about what to do with the remains. They didn't want to burn the corpse in a crematorium, because that would have been too similar to what happened to his victims in Auschwitz. Neither did they want to bury him in Jerusalem, because they were afraid that his evil bones might contaminate the earth. It was never revealed and nobody knows what they finally did with Eichmann's body, whether he remained on Israeli soil or whether he was secretly flown out to some other country like nuclear waste. Perhaps he has now gone to the same place as all his victims. There is no grave and no resting place and it looks like he's become invisible again.

After that I tried to put all the things that happened to me out of my mind. I became the expert at forgetting. I developed a bad memory. I trained myself to go for weeks without remembering anything at all, but then it would come back again through my spine. There was an ache left over from the operation that wouldn't go away. I could still feel it following me around even when I sat down or leaned back against a chair. If anyone touched me I would jump with the sensation of the needle going into my spine again. At night, I had to sleep with my back to the wall. In school I sat at the back of the class. On the bus, too, always the back seat. I even started walking home sideways, like a crab, with my back to the side of the buildings as much as possible. I kept looking around all the time to make sure there was nobody after me, whispering or laughing behind my back.

One day at the harbour, I was in charge, standing at the door of the shed when these girls came up asking questions. Everybody was gone out fishing and I was left to look after the place on my own, leaning against the side of the door just like Dan Turley does all the time. I was the boss and one of the girls came right up and stared into my face, chewing gum.

'How much is your mackerel?' she asked.

I knew she wasn't serious about buying fish, because the other girls started killing themselves laughing. They were falling around the place, sitting down on the trellis, saying lots of other crude things about mackerel and asking how big they were. I didn't answer them. All I could do was smile.

'How much is it for a trip round the island?' she asked, and I could smell the sweetness of the chewing gum in her mouth, she was up that close to my face.

When they got no answer, they started having a big conversation among themselves, putting words into my mouth. They asked if it mattered how many were in the boat and one of them said I wouldn't mind as long as they didn't all sit on top of me at the same time. They wanted to know if it would be a big boat and the others said, big as you like. They asked if I would show them the goats on the island and they answered themselves and said I would catch one of the goats for them so they could ride him around the island all afternoon.

'Don't mind them,' the girl with the chewing gum said. 'Seriously? How much is it for the four of us out to the island?'

I wanted to laugh out loud and have something funny to say back to them. I thought of picking up a mackerel and holding it up to their faces for a laugh, to see what they would say then. But I couldn't do it. I was afraid they would discover who I was. I kept leaning against the shed with my shoulder stuck to the door frame. I felt the pain starting up like a big weight on my spine, as if I was lying face-down with a concrete block on the small of my back. I know that if you say nothing, people will put words in your mouth. They kept guessing what was in my head. They came past me into the shed and walked around examining things.

'You can't go in there,' I said.

'Did you hear that? He can talk.'

But I was a dead-mouth and they walked right in past me. They were taking over the place, touching everything. One of them lay down on Dan's bunk. Others were trying on life jackets, modelling them and dancing around behind me to a song on the radio. They laughed at a calendar with a picture of the Alps that was three years out of date. They saw the spare oars tied up to the ceiling and asked what the white markers were for, playing football or what? They rang the brass bell on the wall. They put a lead weight onto the weighing scales and said it was very heavy. One of them started brushing her hair into a new ponytail and with the sunlight coming in through the window I saw a blond hair floating through the air on its way down to the floor.

They went around saying everything was so dirty. Did I ever think of cleaning the window, for fuck sake. They wanted to know if anyone slept there at night and the others said how could you sleep with the smell of petrol and fish all over you and where was the fuckin' toilet? They kept finding things like oarlocks and asking what the fuck was this for and what the fuck was that for. The others answered and said what the fuck do you think it's for and they all fell around laughing again. They could do what they wanted. They could have taken the petrol out and set the place on fire. I thought of what Packer would have done, how he would have started making up some kind of situation out of it that he could later tell the lads about, offering them some of Dan's pink Mikado biscuits maybe, as long as they didn't mind a few mackerel scales on them as well. Maybe he would have sat down on the bunk with them and shown them Dan's blue mug with years of brown tea-stain inside or cut up a mackerel in front of them until they said, Jesus, let me fuckin' out of here. But I had no way of inventing a life around myself. I had the weakness and I could do nothing until they got bored at last and left of their own accord, laughing and smoking as they walked away up the pier.

And then I could see Dan's boat coming back into the harbour. There was a buzz of motorbikes and the harbour lads were all returning as well and within minutes they were sitting outside the shed again with Packer talking.

'Wait till you hear this,' he said.

He said he was about to tell us the most amazing story. He had just come back in from being out on the water with Dan. They had been pulling up the pots, when they suddenly came across a lobster that had rubber bands already tied around his claws. I'm not joking you, Packer kept saying. There was Dan, complaining about the lobster being less plentiful, and then they came across a lobster that had put his own rubber bands on as if he had given himself up.

I felt the kick in the small of my back. I was waiting for them to turn around and accuse me of being responsible for the empty storage box. I was ready to put my hands up, but nobody mentioned the missing lobster and I began to feel that I was getting away with things at last. I wondered if this was the way life always turned out, that you got caught for the things you didn't do and you got away with the things you should be guilty for, that guilt and innocence eventually balanced themselves out.

Packer said Dan Turley guffawed like a seagull when he saw the lobster with the rubber band coming out of the pot. 'Hooken bloody hell,' he kept saying as he held the lobster in the air. He must have thought somebody had dived down and put the rubber bands on the lobster just to play a trick on him. He was mystified and dumbfounded, looking all around the bay, even away out over the sea across to England to find the culprit, cursing and muttering as if it was all part of the conspiracy against him and even the creatures under the sea were in on it. Dan lifting his white hat to scratch his head and staring at the lobster in his hand as if he had been given a toy without instructions. And then the lads were off again, laughing and holding on to the side of the shed, saying 'hooken this' and 'hooken that', while Dan was standing at the door with his blue mug in his hand, frowning.

Seven

At home, my father calls for another meeting in the front room. It's a summit conference this time, with Onkel Ted present to make sure nobody gets up and starts hitting each other. There's a big silence in the room and lots of tension, everybody afraid to speak first and the gap getting wider all the time until my father gets up to put on a record. I watch him taking the keys out of his pocket and opening the music cabinet. He picks out a record which then suddenly turns out to be the missing John Lennon single.

'This is your record,' he asks. 'Isn't that so?'

I nod my head. I checked the bin a few times and wondered if he had disposed of it some other way, maybe burning it. Instead he kept it with his own collection, along with Bruckner and Verdi and Mendelssohn.

'*Zurück*,' he says, translating the words on the record.

'Yes,' I answer, and I can't help thinking how stupid he makes it sound, as if he wants to kill the words.

'*Na Ciaróga*,' he calls the Beatles in Irish. 'OK, let's listen.'

He does everything with the same care as always. No matter how much he might hate this music, he treats the record with great respect, dusting it off with a special cloth first, even putting on the dust glider before finally touching down the needle. Then he sits down and we listen to the Beatles together.

'Get back to where you once belong, get back, Jojo.'

I see my father looking around as if he can't wait to get the record off his turntable in case it might ruin the needle. It's clear that my mother has been trying to persuade him to do things her way, not with violence but through discussion and compromise. He even gets up to put on the reverse side with John Lennon singing 'Don't let me down', but the whole thing is more and more unbearable to listen to. The only person who seems to enjoy it is my mother, until my father gives her a sharp look and she has to stop tapping her foot. She remembers why the meeting was set up and that there is a serious side to all this. My father takes the record off because it's just too much for him and he thinks the whole system is overheating.

I'm glad when it's over. I'm waiting for him to give his speech about how bad music is like bad food, like chewing gum rotting your teeth, like alcoholism, like taking drugs. I know he feels betrayed, because there's no defence against music. Music is free to travel anywhere across the sea and you can't stop it coming into Ireland and going out again of its own free will. He says I am allowing myself to be corrupted and he wants to remind me of all the good things which we have been concentrating on in our family. He says you have to be careful with music and who I allow myself to be influenced by. My mother says the music is quite nice, but she's heard about how the Beatles have created mass hysteria in young people. We've all seen it on TV, girls screaming and fainting when the Beatles arrived in Dublin. My mother says it reminds her of the way girls were screaming and fainting for Hitler, and she doesn't want me to become brain-washed like that.

'We don't want you to become a *Mitläufer,* a run-along,' she says.

She says it's the worst thing that can happen to you, because it makes you powerless in your legs and you can only run in the same direction as everyone else. It's what happened to the Germans and she remembers how they all became *Mitläufer* under Hitler, with the same thoughts in their heads and the same look in their eyes. My father says it's what happened to the Irish as well, when they started speaking English and were forced to run along after the British. Now we've all just become run-alongs after America, with the same dreams and the same music, and my mother says if you become a run-along, then you don't have much choice. My father and mother both know how hard it is to go in the opposite direction and there are many things in this world they will never run along with. That's why they got married and had an Irish-German family with lederhosen and Aran sweaters, so that we would not be afraid of being different.

When John F. Kennedy arrived on a visit in Ireland, I didn't want to be brainwashed or become a run-along, so I was the only person who didn't go up to the corner house to watch him on TV. I didn't want to be like every-one else, blindly following the leader like they did in Germany under the Nazis. Even though John F. Kennedy was Irish and Catholic and my mother and father liked him for standing up to the Communists who had no religion, I didn't want to be one of John F. Kennedy's followers with American flags and green flags waving at him. When he was assassinated in Dallas one day, I was shocked like everyone else to see the pictures on the front of all the newspapers. I watched my mother pasting those pictures of the motorcade into her diary, but I knew I was not one of his followers because she had already taught me how to be different to everyone else. According to my mother and father, it's alright to be a run-along after John F. Kennedy, or the Pope, or God, or any of the saints, but not somebody like John Lennon.

I don't want to be a follower of John Lennon either, I like his music, that's all. My mother says I have to be careful that I don't get the weakness and lose control of my emotions. Onkel Ted says it's hard to imagine music doing any harm or killing anyone and John Lennon is not mobilizing any armies. My father says John Lennon is an invader and it's more like a cultural war. I wonder what he has planned for the record in the end, whether he's going to break it in his hands in front of me or take it out one day and place it on the garden fire where it will melt down over the top of the weeds a bit like one of the early Beatles haircuts. But this time he's obviously agreed to deal with this matter calmly. My mother has begun to change him and wants him to do things in the German way. She keeps saying that Stefan is coming to visit us soon and we're all going to behave in a very different way from now on.

My father replaces John Lennon in the sleeve and takes out Elisabeth Schwarzkopf. He does all the usual things to keep the dust from interfering with the singing and then her voice comes through the room as if she was standing in the corner and you can actually see her chest lifting up every time she takes in a breath. I can see my mother becoming weightless, floating up above the chair with the music. Onkel Ted as well, all of them floating around the room with the ornaments and vases rising up from the mantelpiece. My father keeps looking at me with a big smile on his face now, because he knows I like Elisabeth Schwarzkopf and I can never deny that. When the record is finished, he stores it away again and turns towards me.

'Now tell me,' he says. 'Which one do you think is better?'

'You can't expect him to give a free answer,' my mother says.

Onkel Ted is there and nobody would dream of losing their temper or disagreeing with each other. My mother wants to put an end to the door-slamming war between me and my father and maybe we should take all the doors off the hinges for a while so we'll get used to the idea that they are not there to make noise with. She starts talking about Stefan again because she can see trouble around the corner.

'Stefan is coming,' she said, but my father holds his hand up to stop her talking.

'Honestly,' he asks me once more. 'With your hand on your heart, which do you think is the better music?'

Onkel Ted says it's hard to make a choice between apples and pears if you like them both. My mother tries to make a joke and says it's a pity we can't hear them both singing together at the same time, doing harmonies.

'What is your choice?' my father demands.

I don't want to barricade myself behind any song. I don't want to think of music as war, but I still feel I have to defend John Lennon, because it's my generation and I want to belong to new music that my father doesn't listen to.

'He's half Irish,' I say. 'His mother is Irish.'

My father doesn't know what to say to that. He knows I'm trying to give the wrong answer again and searches for some hidden meaning to see if I'm deliberately insulting him.

'Stefan is coming,' my mother said. 'Let's be happy.'

'John Lennon,' I continue. 'He's an Irish singer actually. I know the songs are in English, but he's really singing in the Irish language underneath.'

I know it's a bit far-fetched and my father is blinking as if I'm pulling a trick on him. But I carry on telling him that even though John Lennon's middle name is Winston, after Winston Churchill, he is still Irish underneath. He has the Irish language in his heart, even if he can't speak it himself. But I'm no good at persuading my father. I can see him getting angry and he tells me to leave the room. So then I don't care what he does with John Lennon any more because I'm angry myself and all I want to do now is get my own back on him. I get up to leave, but then I want to have the last word before I bang the door behind me.

'He's more Irish than Elisabeth Schwarzkopf,' I say.

I can hear my mother pleading with him to leave it alone. But his footsteps are already thumping along the floor. He rips the door of the front room open again and comes limping out with my mother after him, saying Stefan would be arriving very soon and we didn't want to have a bad atmosphere in the house. Onkel Ted is left standing in the front room, making the sign of the cross, but it's having no effect.

I take flight into the breakfast room where my sisters are making a dress, hunched around a big pattern spread across the table. Ita and Bríd kneeling on the chairs helping Maria to connect up all the pieces of material. Their heads stuck together as if they all had the same sandy brown hair. They look up to see me running around the table with my father right behind me, trying to swing his fist out, scattering the pieces of the dress in all directions. The table is too wide, so he picks up a ruler.

'Come here,' he shouts.

My sisters drop everything and escape out to the kitchen, so it's only my father chasing me around the table now and my mother hanging on to him until he shakes her off.

'Stefan, Stefan,' she keeps repeating.

My father takes off his glasses and stares across the table at me. Right or left. What's his next move, I wonder. It's a game that has often been played before but this time it's serious. My mother lunges at the scissors to remove them. My father is out of breath and I feel sorry for him, because I'm younger and faster. I feel I should give myself up out of kindness, let him get me and then it will be over, but then he decides to push the table towards me, to trap me in one corner. He's already crawling across the dissected dress, reaching out towards me with one hand, so the only thing left to do is to get out under the table, past my mother and up the stairs to lock myself into the bathroom.

After a while, my father comes up and bangs the door with his fist, but it's no use and my mother is finally able to persuade him to go back down. She closes the door of the front room and they discuss the whole thing rationally once more. From the banisters, I can hear my sisters whispering in the kitchen, trying to keep Ciarán happy. In the front room my father's voice was going up and down and I'm wondering what's going to happen to John Lennon now? I can hear my father saying that John Lennon is the last nail in the coffin for the Irish language. My mother says it's only music and that she listened to some pretty stupid pop songs as well in Germany until they were banned. Onkel Ted tells him it's important not to be negative, there's no principle involved and music is not like a hurling match with winners and losers. My mother says it's time to do something big, something generous and imaginative.

They're talking for a long time and it even looks like they've forgotten about it, thinking back over their lives instead and how things have not worked out the way they had imagined it. Maybe they're thinking about the time further back when my father was younger and refused to take advice from anyone because he was afraid it would weaken his ideas. When we were small I can remember him going to the funeral of his cousin Gerald in Skibbereen. My mother often made us pray for Onkel Gerald who was drinking too much and telling too many stories. We were not told how he died, only that it was a tragedy. Some time later we found out that he had taken his own life because his older brother had died in front of his eyes in a drowning accident and he never came to terms with that. My father wanted me to know that as a warning, so I would be afraid of alcohol, because Onkel Gerald could have been a great writer if he hadn't squandered all his stories in pubs around West Cork.

It was one of the biggest funerals ever in Skibbereen, and afterwards all the relatives and friends gathered in the house for sandwiches and tea and whiskey. Everybody was smoking and talking and the small house was crowded, right out to the front door. People kept breaking into tears all the time because Onkel Gerald was a good man who was loved by everybody all the way up to Cork City and Mallow, as far back as Gougane Barra and Bantry. Nobody wanted to believe that he committed suicide in his own home town, when there was so much to live for and he could have been one of the best journalists in Ireland and there was a job open for him any time with the *Southern Star*.

There was an argument at that funeral. When all the people were gathered together, Aunty Eily came over to my father and spoke to him about how he was raising his children. Even though she was heartbroken with grief for her son Gerald, she told my father that what he was doing was wrong. The news was out that my father had stopped allowing his own children to speak English. Even though she had never been to our house and never travelled out of Skibbereen, she had heard it from other relatives who came to visit us from West Cork, saying they had met my mother and tasted her cakes. They said the children were very polite, but that we were afraid. 'Fearful' was the word they used, because each time they asked us a question, we took in a deep breath and were afraid to answer. After the funeral, Aunty Eily told my father that he should stop what he had started before it was too late.

'You'll turn them against you,' she said.

He didn't listen to her. He smiled and said everybody in Ireland would soon be doing the same. He was leading by example and our family was a model for all Irish families in the future. He would not allow anyone to interfere with his mission or say anything about the way that he wanted to run his family.

I can hear Onkel Ted leaving the house and I know they must have come to a decision. My father has been persuaded to do things calmly and they come up the stairs to my room. I see my father holding John Lennon in his hand and handing it back to me like a toy that has been confiscated. He sits down beside me on the bed with my mother on the other side, holding my hand.

'If you want to listen to it,' my father says. 'If you want to listen to any record, just ask me and I'll put it on for you.'

He does not mention the fact that I broke into his music cabinet like a thief. He's going to forget about that. He smiles, trying to put the rage behind him.

'I mean it,' he says, and I know this is a big gesture from him. 'Any time.'

Then he starts confessing something to me. He tells me about the wedding he went to in Skibbereen some weeks back. My father and Onkel Ted both went together in the car, to the wedding of Eleanor and John. He tells me that Aunty Eily was there, too, even though she's very old now. He could see by her face and the way she walked slowly, how much time had gone by, as if the future suddenly comes rushing towards them. At the reception afterwards, everybody was telling stories and singing, but this time it was my father who had tears in his eyes because he sat beside Aunty Eily and told her that he should have listened to her long ago while he had the chance.

'I'm afraid you were right,' he said to her. 'I have turned them against me.'

My father is telling me this himself. He's admitting to me that he was wrong. I want to run out of the room, because I can't bear to think of him like a small boy, with Aunty Eily putting her arms around him. He has tears in his eyes, saying that she told him it is never too late. He says he hopes there is still some time left for us to be friends. He's worried that one of these days I will leave the house and never come back.

I want to be generous to him. I want to tell him that there is no need to feel so betrayed, that the Irish people are still as Irish as they ever were, even if they're all speaking English now. It only means they've become good at acting. They're good at stepping in and out of new roles and new languages, because sometime along the way in the history of Ireland, they became good at being somebody else. I want to tell him that people like John Lennon and Ernest Hemingway and Franz Kafka are all living in the same country now. It's the country I belong to as well, one without any flag. I want to tell him there is nothing to worry about and that music is not like war, but I don't know how to explain that and I don't know if it makes any sense. I don't even know if I believe it myself.

One day, when I was out in the boat with Dan Turley, something happened that made me think nothing made sense any more. We were coming back by the island when I suddenly heard the shout again. Standing on the island was a man holding a bottle in one hand and waving his fist.

'BASTARD' I heard him shout.

It must have been the same man who had shouted Dan's name from the top of the cliff. I could see there was something about him that caused Dan to go even more silent than before. The man on the island was reducing his name to a joke, an insignificant fisherman. Dan wanted him to go away, to drown and disappear. I could see him narrowing his eyes, imagining the man on the island already washed up on the rocks like a dead seal with bite marks punctured in his skin and big black holes where his eyes once were.

Sometimes voices carry really well across the water, depending on how the wind is set and how the waves are facing. When it's calm and there's no wind, the sound carries so far that you can think the whole bay is like a room and you can hear people miles away, just whispering. But this time, the man's voice was not being carried very well and we could hardly hear him. He seemed to have no voice, even though his fist was up in the air and I could see him raging across the water at us. Here and there, the wind carried a word or two across and then whipped it away again.

'Buffaloes,' is all I could make out. 'Papist buffaloes.'

It was a Northern curse, one that you hear on the radio these days. I tried to imagine what would happen if these two men met face to face, what they would do to each other. This time, Dan stared back as if this was some kind of drunken madman who lived out on the island and the less notice you took of him the better. I could see the thimble shape of the Martello tower and the rough grass draped over the island like green tweed. The seagulls were waiting quietly for something to happen. There was a cormorant on a rock spreading his black, oily wings out to dry. I wondered where the island goats had gone to and where they could possibly hide in such an exposed place. I could see the black tide mark all around the edge of the island and I began to imagine that there was also a black rim on the man's lips, from drinking and shouting.

I could see him staggering as he tried to come closer, stepping forward on the rocks as if he was going to walk across the water and kill Dan with his own hands. He began to gesture at us, holding the bottle down to his groin. And still Dan carried on without a word, steering past without seeing him and without hearing him over the sound of the engine. The boat bounced across the waves, cutting through the water and separating the white wash to each side. Dan looked back as if he could stare the man off the island, out of existence. He was standing there, balancing on the rock with the bottle in his hand, shouting but unable to reach us with his anger. He took aim and the bottle crashed on the edge of the island, making a tiny noise like a coin or a brass button falling to the ground.

We kept going towards the harbour and steered right into a cloud. It started raining heavily and my knees were getting wet. Behind us, the island was still in sunshine and the grass was lit up luminous green against the dark blue clouds. We knew the rain would hit the island soon and then we would all be soaked. We kept going with the rain bouncing on the water and Dan looking back at the island until it disappeared from view.

Eight

The first thing we noticed about Stefan was that he didn't eat cake. Nobody had ever refused my mother's baking. Maybe he had better things on his mind and didn't come over to Ireland to eat cake, but it was still hard to think of anyone in his right mind being able to take their eyes off the coffee cake that was specially made for his arrival. It was decorated into sections on top with little squiggled walls of coffee cream which my mother pressed out with her stainless steel syringe, like triangular fields with a haystack in each. She made this cake only on special occasions, when we had a guest, or when there was a birthday to celebrate, so it was like a big prize, standing on the side table with everybody glancing over now and again to make sure it hadn't suddenly disappeared.

We watched Stefan as if we were living at the end of the world and he was the first visitor from outside for a million years. We were like a family cut off by long distance, living on an island so far away that it took him years to reach us. We watched the way he chewed. The way he smiled. Every word he uttered. He spoke German like us, but it was so unusual to see anyone apart from ourselves sitting at the table that we all felt we had been left behind in time. Stefan took the place of Franz at the table, so everybody had to move down one chair to make room, as if he was an older brother who had been missing and had finally come back to us for good. Maria was wearing the new dress that she had made with a pattern of sparks and stars in various colours and my sisters all laughed until they had tears in their eyes whenever Stefan made the slightest joke. Ciarán was examining Stefan's bony cheeks and my mother was asking lots of questions, saying Stefan was tall like his father, Ulrich, but that he had the eyes and the smile of his mother, Käthe. Stefan explained that he was studying medicine, but that he was taking some time off to look around Ireland before it was too late.

When it came to the big moment when my mother cut the cake and placed the first slice on the plate with the silver cake trowel, making sure it didn't fall over on its side, Stefan shook his head and passed the plate back.

'No thanks,' he said with a smile. 'Not for me.'

'No cake,' my mother said, and she was obviously surprised.

She didn't ask him a second time or try to force him the way she would if she was Irish. She offered him Florentines and biscuits instead, but he shook his head at those too. She continued handing out slices of cake to each of us and we stared at the plate in front of us, as if we were doing something strange in our house, something ancient that other people had given up years ago, like being German or speaking the Irish language. I lost interest in the cake myself and my mother thought there was something terrible happening, because I was the one who would always ask for a second slice and now I couldn't even finish the first.

After the table was cleared, my father spread out a map

and started pointing at all the important places in Ireland, giving Stefan information on Irish history, showing him pictures of Robert Emmet on Thomas Street and pictures of the GPO in flames, saying that he would bring him in the car to show him some of these sights. Stefan was listening eagerly and I could see how excited my mother and father were, talking about Ireland. She spoke about the time she first arrived and went cycling on her own up to Lough Derg. My father spoke about Connemara and other places that had to be seen to be believed. It almost looked like they were talking to each other more than to Stefan, trying to convince themselves that these beautiful places still existed, not just in their memory. They took out old photographs and postcards, urging Stefan to travel around as fast as he could before they disappeared.

All the time, while they were talking about Ireland, they were postponing the moment when they would have to discuss the ancient German book, the treasured gift from the time of Gutenberg which Stefan had come to claim back. My mother continued to smile and speak to him in a friendly way to make sure that he felt welcome, but I could see that she was worried underneath and maybe also a little angry or disappointed, too, that nobody remembered what she did for them. In the kitchen afterwards, while my father brought Stefan up to the front room to show him more books about Irish legends, my mother stood staring at the left-over cake as if there was something wrong with it.

'It wasn't always like that in Germany,' she said.

When the war was over, my mother travelled down to Mainz on the train to try and get a job with the Americans. She had to fill in a form called the '*Fragebogen*' like everyone else, to state what organizations she had belonged to and what she had been up to during the war. She had never joined the Nazi party. She had been drafted into the Wehrmacht, but she didn't like to say that she was arrested as a deserter during the last winter of the war, because she thought that might reflect badly on her character.

Her records were in order, so she managed to get work with an American officer and his family in Wiesbaden. Everyone thought she was so lucky, living in a beautiful house on the hill, looking after three small American children, with lots of food at a time when everybody in Germany had nothing. My mother wanted to share this luck and started sneaking food out of the house every evening. When the children were asleep and she had some time off, she got a train to Rüsselsheim to her sister Elfriede and her family. My mother says the two boys, Bernd and Rheinhold, had grey teeth when she first went to see them, and her husband Adam was so thin after being released from captivity that every time he ate even the smallest thing he felt ill again and had to lie down. Rüsselsheim is famous for the big Opel factory where Onkel Adam now works. It's also famous because when the Americans bombed the town during the war the people were so angry that a big crowd of them gathered in the street one day to kill some American pilots who had been captured nearby. After the war, everybody changed and became grateful to the Americans for rescuing them. The Americans went from bombing cities with explosives to bombing cities with raisins, they said. The city of Mainz was heavily destroyed, and my mother remembers seeing the people in the ruins, picking out the bricks and stacking them up to be re-used. She remembers people in the fields going on potato hunts to see if they could find anything that the farmers had missed. She said there was a time of famine in Germany.

The lands around the house in Wiesbaden where the American officer and his family lived were guarded by soldiers and patrols in army jeeps. Every time my mother walked down the hill to the gate, her bag was searched, so she began to conceal food inside her clothes. She held a piece of cheese or meat under her cardigan. Sometimes she hung a small parcel of bread and left-over fat in a small piece of cheesecloth under her arm and walked past the checkpoint knowing that if she was caught, she would lose her job and have nothing.

One day, she had two bars of soap concealed in her stockings, at the back of her legs. She had to walk carefully to make sure the soldiers didn't notice anything. As she walked past the checkpoint, the soldiers smiled and tried to talk to her. She knew they always looked at her legs when she continued on down the hill. She tried to walk as elegantly as possible, but then the bars of soap started slipping down inside her stockings and the soldiers must have thought German women had a funny way of going downhill. She couldn't stop the soap slipping with her hands. Any minute, the soldiers would see two lumps sliding down around her ankles, so she put her foot up on a fence and started adjusting her stockings one by one, as if she was doing it deliberately for them. My mother says they must have imagined everything underneath her dress except the soap. Then she walked away, around the corner out of sight. After that the soldiers were friendly to her and even let her out without checking her bag. Every day, more food was being delivered to the house and every day, more and more was going back out again to feed people in Mainz.

At one time, when the officer and his family went back to America on their summer holidays, the soldiers on guard duty even allowed her to bring people into the house, to help her clean up. There was plenty of food left for three weeks, so my mother invited everybody she knew up to Wiesbaden as if it was her own place. They stayed overnight and slept in all the big beds. And when the food started running out, she decided to use up the last of it in one big party. Stefan's mother and father came. Tante Elfriede and Onkel Adam were there as well. They all went through the rooms and lived for one evening as if they were rich Americans, putting on dresses and suits belonging to the officer and his wife, looking at themselves in the mirror and holding a fashion parade. They lit candles and had a big dinner in the dining room, with cigars from Cuba and French cognac. They put on swing music and danced around the living room. They even spoke in English to each other, my mother says, and they were laughing so much that they often had to hold on to the furniture. But then the party came to a sudden end when the family arrived back early and the house was thrown into a terrible chaos. A phone call came from the station in Wiesbaden to say that they were on their way.

The celebration turned to panic. They turned the music off and ran upstairs to put all the clothes back into the wardrobe. There was such confusion that my mother crashed head-first into her sister on the landing, and even then they could do nothing but hold on to the banisters and start laughing again until they suddenly remembered the trouble they were in. Onkel Adam went around opening all the windows in the house. The others carried things from the dining room into the kitchen, running. My mother says she has never seen the washing up being done so fast in her life. At the last minute, her secret guests all fled out the side door and my mother only had ten minutes to walk around the house closing all the windows again before the family arrived at the door in their big American car.

She doesn't know how they could not have known there had been a party. They must have thought my mother was smoking cigars on her own just to keep a good atmosphere in the house. There was nothing out of place, except that there was not one piece of food left over and the officer's wife said it was about time they got back. My mother was expecting trouble but the Americans were so friendly that when they finally left Germany, they begged her to come and live in their big house in Vermont. They would send her to university. They allowed her time to make up her mind, but she decided to stay close to her own family. They left the address in Vermont and told her that if she ever changed her mind, they would get her a ticket and a visa so she could start afresh in America.

It would have been a good life there. The Americans are very much like the Germans, she says. But then she would never have made it to Ireland. My father would have been an American and we would never have had to learn Irish. We would have been speckled people, but we would never have spoken any German, because it was a time when nobody wanted to be German and nobody wanted to hear German spoken on the street. Sometimes I think about how different our lives would have been with another father, an American father or an Irish father who spoke English to us. My mother imagines what it would have been like, that other life without my father, but she says you cannot regret things too much or you will find yourself going backwards in time and unable to move forward again.

The people in Mainz never forgot how my mother risked everything to keep bringing them food during the war and those famine years. The parents of her school friend Käthe wanted to give her some kind of gift when she finally decided to go away to Ireland. They had no money, and no belongings that could be sold on the black market. My mother didn't want any payment for the help she gave, but Uncle Ulrich's family was so grateful that they decided to give her an ancient book which had belonged to them for hundreds of years.

It was of no value. It could never be sold, nobody would have given even a loaf of bread for it at that time. They knew that my mother liked books, that it would be in good hands. My mother thought it was too precious for her to keep, but they forced her to take it, for all her kindness.

I've seen her holding the book in her hand, leafing through it as if it no longer belongs to her. I've seen her crying, maybe not because she might lose the book, but because what she did that time back in Wiesbaden has no value any more. Maybe that's why she was so shocked that her cake was not accepted, because she remembers the time when people were starving and would have given anything for a piece of that cake. It was hard to believe that there was so much cake around now that people could refuse it. Hard to believe that a piece of cake could ever have been more valuable than a book from the time of Gutenberg. She would never dream of selling it and making money from it. It was one of the first printed books in the world, but that wasn't the same as thinking it would make you rich overnight. When my mother talks about being rich, it's not about money or houses and cars but always about having children and having an imagination, about listening to music and holding precious books in your hand.

Will she give it away or not? One minute she fights back and says she will never let go of this book. She wants to know what right they have to demand such a thing or to claim that she was just keeping it safe for them in Ireland. She feels she has no right to keep it. All she did was help people and that's not something for which you deserve payment. It brought its own rewards and she would be glad to do it again, any time, for nothing. But now she shuts her eyes as if the memory has no value any more, as if something that was still so recent in her own mind had been suddenly wiped away. She was beginning to think it never happened at all. Maybe the book has become so valuable in itself that it has wiped out all memory, all the laughter, all the joy of being alive after the war, all the innocence of that once-in-a-lifetime friendship.

She has thought of hiding it. She has thought of placing it in a vault, with a bank. But in the end it always goes back into the oak trunk with the heavy lid closed down again to keep the past inside.

I've heard my father talking to her late in the evening, saying he will never let anyone take it away from her, because it means as much to him at this stage. It was one of the first things that she showed to him when they met in Dublin after the war. He had lots of things to show her and places to bring her, like Saint Patrick's Cathedral. She had stories to tell him about Germany and he had speeches to make about Ireland, but this book was the first thing that my mother could show him. He remembers leafing through it, knowing that he was holding something that was very close to her heart. It was a sign that she trusted him. He said it was like the ancient books transcribed by the Irish monks, and praised the Germans for inventing printing. It was the only thing that she owned, apart from her clothes, something she had never given out of her hands to anyone before. It was the start of all their luck. It was the start of this Irish-German family and all the stories that we made up along the way. How could she give all that back?

Nine

My father has turned himself into a tour guide for Ireland. It's his country and he's proud to take some days off to show Stefan the most important things about Irish history. He's a very careful driver, keeping both hands on the steering wheel and stopping the car whenever he needs to explain something that cannot be said while driving. He brings us to Kilmainham Jail. We stop outside the GPO on O'Connell Street. We drive to Glendalough to see the round tower. We stand on beaches throwing stones and holding back the waves, as if we've come on holidays from Germany and haven't seen open spaces like this for a long time. We're amazed to see sheep again. We drive into the mountains with the windows open and get the feeling of being lifted up by the landscape, by the emptiness. We stop for lunch and my mother takes out her basket with separate packages of sandwiches. She is still trying to find out what Stefan likes to eat instead of cake, but it remains a mystery to her. We sit in a field with a rug spread out on the grass and everybody laughs because Bríd has begun to chew sideways like the sheep. We go for a walk with grass stalks in our mouths and decapitate wild flowers. My father is not the kind of man who keeps a stem of grass between his lips. Even with his shirt open, he looks like he is thinking about something that still has to be done to improve Ireland, to keep this landscape from disappearing. We climb halfway up a mountain and look back at the small grey Opel Kadett parked like a toy car along the road. We see the houses and the small people of Ireland working in the fields below us. My father holds his arm stretched out in front of him and tells Stefan to look across the landscape with his eyes open, because there are certain things that can only be seen in the Irish language.

'In English,' my father says, 'you can only see as far as the eye can see.'

On the way home he is looking for Echo Gate, driving up and down country roads for a long time saying it can't possibly be gone away. My mother points at lots of gates and tells him to stop so we can shout over them to see if we can hear anything coming back, but he drives on with a determined look on his face until he finally comes to the right place and we all stand shouting across the gate towards the ruins of the monastery. The echo is very clear. We count how many seconds it takes for a word to come back. We shout in German, with the sun going down and the cows looking up, wondering what we're saying. It's a perfect echo each time, as if the fields know our language. A whole family shouting back at us with great excitement, as if they had been waiting there for centuries, and this is the first time somebody has come to the gate who understands them. Our voices have come out from under the mossy stones and start calling back, hoping we don't leave again.

'How are you all over there and how did you know we were coming?' my father shouts in Irish. When the echo comes back, my mother says it must be Irish because who else would answer a question with another question? The sky changes in layers of yellow and purple and deep grey. We can see the dark outline of the ruins fading against the land. Stefan is barking like a dog. Ciarán climbs the gate and Maria stands beside him, singing a do-re-mi ladder of notes that stands up against the sky and we're like a family laughing at ourselves in the mirror. Even when we get back into the car and drive away, my mother's voice is still laughing around the ruins after it gets dark.

Each time we arrive home again, my father sits down to make notes on the trip, how many miles have been travelled and how much petrol was used. My father is not the kind of man who washes his car every weekend, but he is the kind of man who keeps a little notebook where he records every detail and tries to get as many miles per gallon as possible. He checks the pressure in the tyres before and after every journey, and at the end of the long trip back from Echo Gate, he lets the air out and replaces it with fresh air, until Stefan tells him very politely that it doesn't make any sense and the quality of the air inside the tyre is not what matters. Stefan can say things to my father that we would be afraid to say, because he doesn't like to be criticized by his own family.

I become a tour guide myself and take Stefan out fishing with Franz. Stefan cooks the mackerel we catch with a funny new Irish recipe given to him by Dan Turley, grilling the fish and sprinkling cornflakes on the top. At last, my mother finds something that Stefan likes to eat instead of cake and begins to bake barm brack. We play cards and chess and go to the field every day to play football. Stefan is so clever with his feet that other boys come to watch and join in because football needs no language. He can make the ball disappear from under their feet and they start calling him Beckenbauer. So it's

Eichmann and Beckenbauer and Hitler playing together in the football field until Stefan gets fed up with his new name.

I showed him the place where they found the body of a murdered woman. I brought him to the spot on the seafront where the body of Peggy Flynn was discovered. It was in the papers and everybody was talking about it for months in the shops. They said it was too nice a location for something like that to happen and now it was changed for ever, as if the landscape would never heal. They said it was terrible to think of her being found dead with her face down in the water and her hair waving around like seaweed, with crabs and sea-lice crawling over her. Some of them could not even utter the word murder and called it a tragedy, as if they wanted to restore her dignity. Special prayers were said at Mass on Sundays. The priest called it a shock to the core of the heart. It was un-Irish and they believed it was coming from somewhere else, from abroad, from places that had no religion, where people had no morality. They were worried that the murderer was never found and it frightened them to think it could be somebody normal walking around the streets of Dublin like anyone else.

Even long after the body was taken away and the Gardai had carried out all their investigations, they still kept people away from the scene. A squad car was parked there with two officers looking out towards the sea, as if they were expecting the perpetrator to come back and look for something he might have left behind or dropped accidentally.

I knew I was the murderer. I had not actually murdered Peggy Flynn, but how could I be sure I might not murder somebody in the future some time? I could not trust myself. When the squad car eventually disappeared from the seafront, I started going down every day like a perpetrator returning to the site of the crime. I stood there and knew exactly what it was like for the person who murdered her. He must have thought he got away with it and that he could return to the scene like any other normal person, but he was obsessed by her. Not a day went by without her name coming back to him. His own deed was like rat poison turning his stomach inside out. I stood looking out over the rocks where she was found, with the waves moving the seaweed backwards and forwards and the seagulls on the rocks keeping watch. I thought of her name, Peggy Flynn. I could hear her voice in my head, talking to me and asking me what the matter was. I thought of the way she looked, wearing a tweedy skirt, above the knees. I saw her laughing and making faces at her friends. I saw her getting off work and walking through the streets of Dublin where I go to school, waiting for a bus on Parnell Square, searching in her handbag and looking sideways at me, throwing her head back to get the hair out of her eyes. Again and again, throwing her head right back and smiling at me, before her hair slowly started dropping down over her forehead like a slow curtain in the cinema.

My mother said I should stop and not go down there any more. She gave me a book called *Crime and Punishment*, and I wondered if she got it from Onkel Ted, because after reading it, you can never believe in God again as long as you live. The book is about a student in Moscow who murders an old woman living alone in the same building. Reading it makes you think how easy it is to take somebody's life. And maybe that's why they gave me the book, because they want me to know that your crime stays with you for the rest of your days, like a partner who never leaves your side.

Up to the time I read that book, I thought murder was wrong because everybody said it was wrong. But then I started thinking about how morality was invented in the first place, way back in time, before there was anything like police and courts and the ten commandments. How did people decide that killing was wrong? They must have discovered that murder was impractical because dead people had relatives and friends who would come looking for revenge. It would keep going around in circles, people killing and punishing each other into infinity. Maybe that's what a conscience is, I thought, imagining the consequences of your actions. Maybe that's how compassion started in the first place, people imagining what other people felt and how you would feel if the same thing happened to one of your own people. I thought about all the people like Eichmann who had no feelings at all. But even people with no feelings and no conscience, they still had an ego. Every criminal wants to be loved and respected. Even if they don't want forgiveness, they still want recognition. They don't want to be forgotten, because the loneliness of being a murderer is too hard to live with.

At the end of the book there's a good feeling because Raskolnikov sits on a pile of logs looking out at the river. It's a wide river with nothing beyond it, only the steppe. He's in prison in Siberia and he still has to serve seven years of his sentence, but he can see that at the end of those seven years, he will have paid for his crime. He's happy because he hears the nomads singing on the far side of the river and he thinks time has moved on and his guilt has come to an end. He knows that forgiveness is coming and soon he will become a new person.

My mother said murder was a failure of the imagination. I could feel the memory of war and fear and regret in her words. She told me she read a famous line by a writer called George Steiner who said history had taught us that you could live a happy life with your family and listen to Bach in the evening and go out the next day to commit the most horrible crimes in Auschwitz. She said Bach was not the problem and hoped I would always have enough imagination left to remember what it's like to be inside somebody else's shoes. She said it was not difficult to murder somebody. It was the opposite. It's hard not to murder somebody. And it's even more difficult to make up for it afterwards.

'The hardest thing is to un-murder somebody,' she says. 'You need a big imagination to be able to do that, to bring somebody back to life. As long as a dead person is remembered by one single person, they are not quite dead yet. You can keep somebody alive for ever in your memory.'

When I showed Stefan the place where Peggy Flynn was murdered, he didn't say much. There was nothing for him to say and he just stared at the rocks without asking any questions. I noticed him going quiet in the days after that and it wasn't long before he announced that he was leaving to travel around the country on his own. My mother was surprised that he didn't want to talk about the ancient book which he had been sent to collect. She didn't want to leave it until he came back from his tour, but when she brought up the subject, Stefan seemed to have no interest at all, only in maps of Ireland.

On the last day before he left, I went swimming with him. I brought him up to a secret place that I had found some time ago and shown nobody else in the world. Up there on the hill, by the big terrace of white houses overlooking the bay, there was a small lane leading down to the rocks. It was overgrown, but I got a stick and hacked a path through, until we came out at the bottom and we could see the whole bay with the long sandy beach running all the way into the distance. We could see crowds of people on the beach and the train running along the coast. We swam off the rocks and I saw that Stefan had a mole on his back, like a birthmark. I could see a thin black line of hair running down from his belly button and disappearing into his togs. His chest was strong and he was a great swimmer.

We sat down in a sunny place where nobody ever went and we had the whole bay to ourselves. The rocks were hot, like granite radiators. I could smell the dried seaweed around us like the smell of packet soup. When I pushed a rock aside it revealed all the sea crawlers and jumping sand-fleas underneath. Stefan threw a few rocks around just to hear them clacking against each other. We didn't need to talk, but then he started asking me about my father, wondering why I went along with his rules and why he would still not allow us to speak English. He wanted to know if it was always like that in our house, listening to pop songs on the radio in secret. I could not answer him. I didn't know how to talk about my father to people outside the family. Other lads all called their fathers 'the old man' or 'the oul fella', but I didn't like it. I didn't know how to be disloyal.

'I don't speak to my father,' Stefan told me.

It sounded like he was encouraging me to do the same.

'I haven't spoken to him in a year,' he said.

'Why?' I asked.

'He saw people being executed.'

I asked him where and he looked out over the water

as if he could remember seeing it himself with his own eyes.

'Women. Naked women,' he said. 'He was in the war, in the East, in Russia.'

I didn't know how to ask him anything else. I wanted to go away for a while and come back with more questions, even though I knew he was leaving and it might be too late. He spoke about his own father as if he was a murderer. I thought of my father and began to wonder if he was a murderer, too, and wanted to kill people for Ireland. I thought of how I would stop talking to him, only that my mother would start whispering into my ear, saying that if I stop talking to my own father, I will not be able to talk to myself either.

We sat watching a small fleet of yachts coming around by the island, all leaning in the same direction. Above us every now and again a train passed by along the edge of the cliff and disappeared, rushing into the tunnel with a sudden muffled sound. Seagulls threw themselves off the face of the cliff and balanced in the air. In the big terrace of white houses, there was a woman leaning out the window looking far off at the sugarloaf mountain. Stefan told me that he was going to get as far away as possible from his father and from his country. I was afraid of what he was saying. I had never heard anyone speaking so openly about themselves before. He said he had a girl-friend in Mainz and she was very beautiful. He told me that he had slept with her and it was something he would never forget. But it was all wrong, he said, because he had lost all sensation in his heart. He said he felt like a murderer with no feelings. He was like the un-dead and that's why he had come to Ireland, so he could touch things and breathe again. We didn't look at each other while he was saying all this. We kept our eyes on the water, on the yachts, and the seagulls who looked like they were imitating the yachts, racing each other at an angle in the air above us.

Ten

The harbour is shaped like an Irish harp with the road running straight along one side, a bow-shaped pier along the other side, and a perpendicular pier at the top where the gap opens up for the harbour mouth. All the ropes tying the boats down to their moorings are the strings, sometimes tight, sometimes loose. The road is bordered by granite bollards and looping chains. At the bulging side of the harp, the granite pier is built up with cottages and fishermen's huts. Most of the sheds are no longer owned by fishermen, apart from Dan Turley's which is the last one on the pier, closest to the harbour mouth. The bottom end of the harp is the shallow end of the harbour with a slip for small boats to enter the water, while right across from Dan Turley's shed, there is a crane where larger boats are lowered with straps and you can hear the wood creaking with the strain. They say the harbour was constructed around a natural cove which had been used for smuggling long ago until the road was built. There are small working harbours like this all along the coast, as well as the big ferry harbour with its two granite arms reaching out and a lighthouse at each end. Our harbour is used mostly for pleasure boats now and for fishing, mackerel, lobster and crab. If it rains, we all hang around inside Dan's shed, smoking and talking, watching the pier being washed clean until it clears up and you can see the steam rising all around. If the sun shines for a while, you can feel the heat left behind in the granite long after it's dark. Sometimes Packer goes up to the shop and comes back with a half-dozen ice pops to share out and everybody laughs at the way Dan Turley eats his like a small boy, biting off a big chunk and concentrating hard while he's juggling it around in his mouth before he finally swallows it and gets the brain freeze.

On Saturdays, every boat from every harbour seems to be out. The whole bay is full of yachts with white sails and coloured, bulging spinnakers, like one big washing line criss-crossing the bay. We're busy all afternoon, bringing people out to the moorings, rushing for those who give the best tips. Packer knows everybody by name, but he remembers them mostly by some personal feature, like the man who speaks with a deep voice that sounds like applause coming out of his mouth. There's the man Packer calls The Abbreviator because he keeps dropping vital words and just says 'luck' over his shoulder. There's another man called Banjo because he keeps humming the same tune, always 'I come from Alabama with a banjo on my knee...' He goes through every variation of the Alabama banjo tune, humming, whistling, huffing and blowing, even deliberately suppressing the melody and just hissing the beat because he can't stop it coming through some way or another. Packer says he must keep it up even when he's eating his dinner at home, and he probably gets into bed at night with his wife, still yawning the same bloody tune like some terrible kind of musical motor neurone disease.

There's a well-known newspaper journalist with bushy

eyebrows who goes out in a small boat that's always leaning to one side. There's a TV presenter who speaks in Irish and English all the time, switching back and forth in mid-sentence like a balancing act between both languages. There's a man and his wife who go out together in the matching white Aran sweaters and life jackets, so Packer calls them The Coordinates. There's a doctor with a pipe who leaves a sweet tobacco smell floating after him around the harbour and brings out a big bunch of children from the inner city. There's one man who is remembered only because he once tied up his launch along the outer pier and came back from a drink in the Shangri La Hotel to find the tide gone out and his boat hanging high and dry on the ropes. There are lots of people who have no boats of their own so they take out our boats regularly, like the man who looks like Henry Kissinger with a fake suntan. The harbour lads say 'How's Vietnam going?' as soon as he's out of earshot. There's a woman who goes out to the island to practise singing and the harbour lads start doing scales. There's a plain-clothes policeman who works in the drugs unit who never actually goes out on the water at all and is more interested in coaching football teams, but he comes down to talk to Dan for a while, using all the cool Garda lingo like 'over and out' and 'mission impossible'.

And then there's Tyrone with sandy hair and his cigarette in his mouth, carrying an engine in one hand and a bag in the other. The whole harbour seems to fall silent when he is around and you know there's trouble in the air. This is the man who shouts at Dan, the man who threw the bottle on the island. Only this time he walks by without a word and it's Dan Turley who is muttering abuse after him.

'There he goes,' Dan says under his breath. 'Tyrone the brave. Take a good look at him, lads.'

Packer says you can smell the resentment on the pier, like old fish bait in the sun, covered in bluebottles. He says Dan is a Catholic from Derry and Tyrone is a Protestant from Belfast, so it's like having our own mini-troubles right in front of our eyes. Tyrone turns around to give Dan a filthy look. He mutters something back, something maybe with the word 'drowning' in it, or maybe it's just the way we hear it and think everything turns into a curse. He walks away and Dan steps out onto the pier to do a bit of silent Irish dancing after him. And then we're all laughing because the harbour boys are repeating Dan's words again until they have to hold their stomachs. We're on the winning side now and it's Tyrone making his way down the steps into his boat with the harbour laughter behind him.

Everybody is out on the water, fishing, sailing, or just drifting, and it's Packer and me patrolling the bay to make sure none of our boats are in trouble. We forget about the time they tried to cut through our friendship, when Packer would not talk to me. That's all over now and he says we're going to do something big to make up for it.

It all started when I got friendly with Packer at school. One day on the way home, we walked into an amusement arcade on O'Connell Street to try our luck at the slot machines. We couldn't lose. We were the biggest winners since the beginning of time, putting more and more of Packer's money into the machines. We laughed every time we were lucky and laughed even more when we lost. We could already feel the envy of others who didn't come with us that day, because the pennies just kept spitting out for us without stopping. No matter what machine we tried, the symbols lined up for us. It was three lemons or three bars and we kept winning more and more until at one point, we won the big jackpot. It was star-star-star, lined up in a row. Bells were ringing and pennies started cascading out into the tray for us. The women at the other one-armed bandits looked around, wondering why they were sitting at the wrong machine. It seemed like Packer had all the luck in the world.

Then the manager came running out and one of the women told him that it was her machine, that she had been at it all day long and smoked an entire packet of cigarettes while putting pennies into it. Her name was written on that jackpot.

'Am I right, Mary?' she said, turning to her friend. She said it was her money in that machine and now we came along, cool as you like, and just stole it from her. Robbers, she called us. So the manager threw us out for being under age. Packer argued with him but there was nothing we could do. He wouldn't give us the money that we had won fairly and just ushered us out towards the door with all the women sitting at the machines staring at us. Some of them had cigarettes hanging from their lips and ash on their clothes. Some of them had little plastic buckets of pennies between their knees and some of them kept putting pennies into the slot and pulling the arm without looking, as if they couldn't stop. At the door, Packer turned around and stared back at them all for a moment.

'Vile and ordinary,' he said slowly and triumphantly.

They didn't care. I started laughing and the manager pushed me out. We both stumbled forward into the crowd passing by on the pavement.

'Don't fuckin' show your faces around here again,' the manager shouted, and the people on the pavement stepped away, wondering what kind of thugs we were. Packer said it was the biggest injustice ever. There was nothing we could do, nobody we could complain to, so we started getting our own revenge on the world, going around annoying people and coming home late, locking the train door when people were trying to get on, shouting at the station master and causing lots of trouble until the complaints started going into the school.

My mother was worried about me becoming a run-along. I would end up being a *Mitläufer* after Hitler, and the same thing would start all over again, everything the Germans went through with the Nazis. She wanted me to have a mind of my own, to stand out from the crowd and not to be like everyone else, running along after Packer. My father said I had been brainwashed. There was a lot of talk about indoctrination and bad influence. People were being brainwashed all over the Soviet Union, just as they were brainwashed under the Nazis as well. Now they were being brainwashed in snooker halls and coffee shops and amusement arcades all around Dublin. Places like Murrays basement record store and Club Caroline and Club Secret became famous for young people becoming powerless with alcohol and drugs. They were being hypnotized and had no minds of their own. They were dancing like puppets to the music, with no control over their own arms and legs. Onkel Ted had to come out to the house and we sat in silence together in the front room. After a long time, he told me he had been reading a book about crowds and power which described everybody being obsessed with privacy and making sure other people didn't come too close.

People saw each other as a threat, until they were in a crowd, that is, then they felt safe. People who wouldn't say hello to each other in a million years were suddenly all friends going in the same direction.

'Be careful of crowds,' he said to me.

He made the sign of the cross but we both knew that it was too late and I was already lost. I told him I had been brainwashed by my father into speaking Irish. I had been brainwashed into being German as well and now I wanted to be brainwashed out of all that as fast as possible. Come on, brainwash me, I was saying to John Lennon, to Packer, to anyone coming along the street, to any movie that was being shown in the cinema at the time. I needed to live outside my family. I needed to be neutral and I went into hiding, behind Packer. I started to live inside his life.

My father said I had become a slacker, which is the same as what he used to say in his speeches on O'Connell Street about all the Irish people. He said I had become a borrowed personality, like some garden tool that people lend to each other and never give back. At school, it was no better, with all the brothers and teachers saying I was a nobody and a waster. It was funny because I took it as a compliment.

One day Brother K started talking to us in class about career guidance. He wanted to be a progressive educationalist and to spout on to us about how important it was to streamline. But it wasn't long before his talk on career options became a big warning on what might become of us if we didn't keep working hard. He turned it into a forecast of what we would all end up doing with our lives. He said Metcalf would be sweeping the streets. De Barra – bus conductor. Hurdail – civil servant. Mac an Easpaig

– travelling salesman. He went around the whole class one after the other like a fortune teller, gazing into the future, imagining us in suits and ties, carrying briefcases with brochures for new refrigerators inside. He imagined some of us staring out from the scaffolding on building sites in Birmingham. He said De Pluncead would be a nightwatchman in a place called Chiswick, because he was always falling asleep in class. He said Delaney would be driving one of those red double-decker buses in circles around Trafalgar Square. O Cionnaith – playing football for the British in Doncaster. He said most of us would have to emigrate because we were too stupid to do anything else. We were knowledge-resistant, like water-proof rain-gear, unable to absorb education. Those who stayed at home would do no better. O'Bradaigh – making sausages like his father. Calthorpe did all right because he would become a famous surgeon wearing a bow tie. MacElroy did even better as a nuclear physicist and Lennihan got the best career of all as a pilot, because it meant he would be smoking Rothmans.

Brother K selected my friend Packer out for special attention, predicting that he would become a Hollywood actor.

'Every class has a Packer,' he said. 'Every country has a Packer. Every moment in history has a Packer. He is your Greek God of clever words, the God on whom you pin your empty hopes. You nonentities, you will follow this man over the cliff because he fills the void inside your biscuit-tin heads.'

When it came to me, Brother K seemed to have nothing left to say. He searched in his head and could not think of any occupation or vocation that would be suitable for me, not even a meat-packer, or a greyhound trainer.

He said I would be nothing. A true nobody. A waster and a tramp.

'I'm afraid it's park benches for you,' he said, and the entire class let out a roar.

Every summer my father made us stay at home and study. When we got our summer holidays and everybody else was free, my father gave my brother Franz and me three days off, but then we had to go back to school in our house to study the next year's course in advance. He wanted us to be brilliant students and drew up a school timetable for us, with maths and history and little breaks in between. While everyone else was out swimming, we had to do our essays and learn things off by heart. He would phone my mother from the office to ask her how we were getting on. He had a copy of the timetable in his briefcase, so he knew what subject we should be working on at any time. My mother became the enforcer, but then she started letting us get away with it. And one time, when Tante Minne was over on a visit, she took us down to Glendalough for the day and my father was waiting at the door when we came back, saying that we had taken time off and we now had to catch up what we had missed, even though it was after nine in the evening. So then there was a big row between Tante Minne and my father. She said that if he was going to insist on us sitting down to do our homework at that time of the night, in the middle of the summer holidays, then she would not stay there, she would leave and get a room in a hotel somewhere.

After that, my mother helped us to escape. Every time my father rang from the office, she said we were studying like good boys, even though we were outside. By the time we went back to school again after the summer, I hated it so much that I refused to do anything. My mother still helped me out and allowed me to get out of school now and again to go to the pictures in secret. I went to see *Alfie* and *The Graduate*, and *Valley of the Dolls*. But then I was caught and a new door-slamming war started.

My father blamed Packer. My mother wanted everything done without violence, so she sat down in the kitchen with all the sticks from the greenhouse one day and broke every one of them into little pieces over her knee with my sister Bríd crying because my mother was hurting herself, undoing all the lashes back through history. I became unpunishable.

'Do you want to be a nobody?' my father kept asking.

'Yes,' I answered. 'That's exactly what I want to be, a nobody.'

'So you want to stop learning,' he said.

I told him I wanted no more information. I wanted to be blank, without knowledge, which is the worst thing you could ever say to my father because he was a schoolteacher once and he struggled to get an education. He kept saying knowledge gives you strength and I kept saying knowledge made you weak and guilty, until he got so furious that he threw a bowl of stewed apple over my head. My mother had made it from cooking apples grown in our garden. I could see four or five black cloves floating under the surface of the green, semi-solid substance, like mines ready to explode. I saw the steam rising because it was still too hot to serve. He was blinking fast behind his glasses and when I told him I want to remain empty-headed, he picked up the bowl of *Apfelkompott* in the middle of the table and stood up to dump the whole lot on my head. I could feel the warm pudding sliding down around my ears. I sat there with the rest of the family looking at me while the stewed apple slipped in around my neck and I felt like a hero who had won the argument.

My mother stood up and said she should make *Apfelkompott* more often since we liked it so much. She was angry and the house was full of door slamming. My father then got the idea that I should go to see a psychiatrist, I was in danger of destroying the family. I refused to go and said it was him who needed a psychiatrist, but then he threatened to throw me out of the house. I had a choice, to go for treatment or become homeless. I was afraid that I was no longer in control of my own thoughts and that I was going mad. I thought I would end up mentally disturbed in an asylum with lots of people who had no power over their own minds. Once I was classified as mental, there would be no turning back.

I know my mother was not to blame for this, because she was not able to go against him. She didn't want me to lose my imagination, so she begged me to make a compromise, which was not like capitulating entirely. She said I only had to go and talk to the man, no harm would come of that. So I went to the psychiatrist and sat there listening to this man with big lips asking me questions about myself. What does he know about being German, I thought. And when he started asking me stupid questions about what I thought of girls, I told him to fuck off. I thought he would write home and my father would find out he was paying a lot of money for somebody to listen to me telling him to fuck off, but luckily it was a confidential conversation and the letter my father got only informed him that the psychiatrist could make no great progress.

Then one day Packer stopped talking to me. I waited for him as usual in the morning on the way to school, but he just walked past me and got on the train. I tried to talk to him but he wouldn't even look at me. He closed the door and I had to get on another carriage when the train was already moving. Suddenly, he stopped being my friend. I saw him every day at school with everybody listening to his stories, everything was still the biggest and the best, but I was no longer included. He pretended I didn't exist any more. If I approached his group or tried to listen to what he was saying, he just walked away as if he couldn't bear to be in the same room as me.

I even went to the Waverly Billiard Hall to see if he was there one day after school, but he never looked at me once, just concentrated on his game.

'What's wrong?' I asked him. 'What did I do?'

Then he dropped his cue and walked out as if he was never going to play snooker in his life again.

I couldn't prove it, but I knew that my father must have secretly sent a letter to Packer's mother to say that her son was turning me into a run-along. Packer was afraid of his mother in the same way that I was afraid of my father, so maybe she told him not to have anything to do with me. Everybody in the world is afraid of Packer's mother. Once she cut through the television cable with a pair of scissors to make him do his homework. So maybe my father and her got together to cut through our friend-ship cable, because she got Packer to turn his back on me and walk away without ever looking back. She must have sent a letter back to my father saying that I was turning her son into a monster and a mountebank, because some-times it's the run-along that gives a leader the courage to do all kinds of terrible things that he would never even dream of getting away with by himself.

After that I had no crowd to belong to. I heard the boys at school repeating some of the amazing things that happened to Packer and what a great life he was having. But I was no longer part of it. I was walking home sideways again, with my back to the wall. I was a nobody and everybody was looking at me as if I was a dead cat. I knew what it was like to be mentally disturbed and have nothing to say. I had no life and no inner dream and no story for myself.

Every time I think about this, I want to kill my father. I tell my mother that I'm not going to be kept in the wardrobe any more, like his own father, the sailor with the soft eyes. I'm going to break out and escape down to the harbour. If he tries to stop me, I will kill him and make him disappear, like his own father. My mother tells me not to repeat the mistakes of history. If you kill your father, you will kill yourself as well. If you hate your father you will hate yourself for ever. Instead of fighting with him openly, my mother encourages me to find my freedom elsewhere, by going to films, reading books, and not through anger.

So now I've become sneaky, doing things behind my father's back. I go up to his bedroom while he's out at work. I open his wardrobe and look at the big picture of the sailor with the soft eyes inside. He must feel the same way that I felt when Packer was not talking to me, frozen out. I wonder what he did that was so terrible. Nobody deserves to be locked away from the world like this, and I know what it's like to be in that wardrobe, because I was trapped in there once as a child. I look at the face of the sailor and wonder why he joined the British navy, and how he is now being punished. It's hard to get that out of my head. He was a fisherman before he joined up. Now I'm a fisherman, and maybe we're friends and I've taken his place.

I want to rescue him. I cannot take his picture out, so I do something that will make it less lonely for him in there in the dark. I take the John Lennon disc that my father gave back to me. I can't ever play it anyway, so I hide it in the wardrobe behind the picture of the sailor. Nobody is going to know it's there, but it's a great feeling to have a secret, to know that my grandfather has a friend to keep him company. It's John Hamilton and John Lennon talking to each other and whispering in the dark. It's John Hamilton joining the Beatles and singing harmonies along with John Lennon in the wardrobe at night, while my father is trying to get to sleep.

They're singing, Back in the US, Back in the US, Back in the USSR...

Eleven

One day at school, I got my chance to show that I was not invisible. I made up my mind to do the thing that everybody was most afraid of. The instrument of torture. I decided to steal it.

Without Packer on my side, they kept laughing at my brother and me for being half Irish and half German. It was weird, they said, like a big contradiction, because the Irish got the shit kicked out of them by the British and the Germans kicked the shit out of the Jews. We were innocent because we were Irish and we were guilty because we were German. Victim and perpetrator at the same time. They couldn't deal with this and said they wanted to kick the shit out of us. I was careful, trying to stay out of sight, walking home sideways with nobody behind me, but then they got Franz. It was as if my brother was part of my weakness. They rammed his head up against the railings of the Garden of Remembrance and he came home with blood down the back of his shirt. My father sent a letter to the school the following day to say nobody had the right to do that. We were living in a free country now and people should be allowed to go about their business without being called Nazis and being punished for nothing.

Brother K had always applied the rule of pre-emptive

punishment. He punished the innocent and the guilty together, to prevent revenge attacks and faction fighting going on into infinity. But it seemed not to be working, because everybody was copying his methods. So he smiled and reminded us all of the concept of referred pain. One boy gets a lash and everyone else feels it. Sometimes it was the innocent people getting all the punishment and the guilty ones getting off, but referred pain was still a great deterrent, the lesser of two evils.

Brother K rounded up all the boys who had been involved in the incident and said he would make an example of them. In a big speech, he explained that what happened outside the school could not go on and he was going to punish them so hard that everybody in the whole school would feel the pain. He said he never wanted to read a letter like that from my father again. My brother never wanted revenge. He didn't like to see anyone punished. He just wanted to put it behind him and move on. But Brother K made us watch each lash. It went on for ever. And when the perpetrators had received their punishment, Brother K called Franz forward and explained that it was his duty to punish him as well. To prevent any bitterness and any further victimizing, he was obliged to give him the same amount of lashes as his tormentors got.

Franz cried, maybe not as much with the pain but with the sheer humiliation. Everybody knew this was unfair. The story went around the whole school and I could see everyone laughing as if it was the funniest thing that ever happened. Franz put it behind him, but I could not move on. Even though I was lucky enough not to be punished just for being his brother, I could not forget the injustice of it. It gave me the rage and I wanted to kill Brother K, to stick an axe into the back of his head. At night I stayed awake and imagined how I would kill anyone who laughed at us, bash all their heads against the railings. I was like my father and I could not stop planning ways of winning. I had to balance the scales. The punishment of my brother had to be put right.

I decided to steal the instrument of injustice. Every day I kept an eye on where Brother K kept it, sometimes in his pocket, sometimes in his briefcase. Then the opportunity came quite unexpectedly when I was going down the stairs to the lavatory one afternoon and spotted Brother K's briefcase outside the principal's office with the door ajar. There was nobody around. I knew he would be coming out the door any minute. I knew it was a big crime, bigger than anything that happened before in the school. I was finished if I was caught. But then I went ahead without thinking. I didn't even have to open the briefcase because the instrument of punishment was sticking out. I put it under my jumper and ran away with the heat rising into my head. I made it down to the bicycle shed where I hid it temporarily. When I got back to my class, everybody said I looked pale and sick. Later on, after school, I went back to the bicycle shed and put it into my schoolbag. I didn't talk to anyone, just brought it with me to find a safer hiding place. The school we go to in the city is situated right beside the Municipal Art Gallery, so I walked right in and started looking at the different paintings. In the end, I decided to place the instrument of torture on top of the gilded frame of a Dutch woman.

The next day, Brother K started a big inquiry. All classes were called off until further notice, until the perpetrator was found, until somebody owned up and took responsibility for the crime. For two days we did nothing except wait in line to be questioned in an empty room.

He called each boy in separately, then sat in silence for a long time, staring at him, hoping that he would break. Brother K had a shiny red face and an upper tooth missing, a molar that left a black gap whenever he smiled. But he kept his mouth firmly shut, with a serious grimace, just waiting. He had all the time in the world, he told me. I heard the buses going by outside and the seagulls on the roof of the school. We waited and waited. I knew he had the power on his side and that I had only the weakness of being always guilty and having no friends in the world. But then I knew I also had some of the power on my side, because he had carried out the biggest injustice ever on my own brother. For once it was good to have no friends and to be totally alone in the world, because it makes you a better criminal. I didn't have to tell anyone what I had done, not even Franz. I was only waiting for the moment when I could tell Packer, so that he would be friends with me again. He would turn the whole thing into a great legend and tell the story like it was a film. He would introduce me to all kinds of new people, saying here is the man who stole the instrument of torture, the thing that was most hated by anyone who ever went to school.

'I know you did it,' Brother K said.

I went red in the face immediately, as if he had switched on a light. I was shaking and started getting sick in my stomach with fear. I was ready to collapse and make a confession. But then I wondered how he could be so sure it was me, unless he saw me actually taking it or hiding it in the Municipal Gallery next door. I said nothing. I guessed that he was saying the same to every other boy in the school, waiting for the guilty person to crack. He spoke my name slowly, then repeated his accusation.

'You did it.'

'No I didn't,' I said.

'You're only making it worse for yourself,' he said.

I was compounding everything, the lie that covers up the initial crime. It would spiral out of control in a vicious circle of lies and deceit. He stared at me for a long time, then smiled. I even smiled back until he suddenly went very serious again.

'I'm giving you a last chance to think about it,' he said.

He finally told me to step outside while he called in the next boy. I was certain that he knew everything just by divine inspiration. I became desperate and thought of ways to undo what I had done. I imagined that none of this was happening, that my brother never got attacked outside school in the first place. I started undoing everything in history as well, all the things that happened during the Nazi times. I tried to imagine that there was no such thing as the Irish famine. No war over the Suez Canal, no invasion of Hungary, no Vietnam. I wanted to be able to stop houses burning. Stop ships sailing out, stop trains leaving the station.

I thought of slipping out to the Municipal Gallery and retrieving the instrument of torture, replacing it quietly while nobody was looking, leaving it to be found by other boys on the floor of the classroom. But it was too late for that. I prepared a confession. After two days, I was ready to crack. Then Brother K made an unexpected announcement. He said he had drawn up a shortlist of five key suspects. He was not giving out the names yet, in order to allow the perpetrator one last chance to come forward voluntarily. There was still time, he said. After lunch, he would name the five suspects and punish the living daylights out of them so that the pain would be felt all over the school and through the streets of Dublin, down O'Connell Street and out into the suburbs. The pain would go nationwide. Four of them might be innocent, but it was important not to allow the real culprit to get away.

During lunch break, I heard the other boys saying to each other that they would absolutely crucify the guy who did it. If he didn't own up and save the innocent from being punished, he was going to need a wheelchair. I was caught both ways. I was certain that Brother K was bluffing and that he had no idea who did it. He was lashing out indiscriminately. But the alternative might be even worse, if the boys suspected that I was responsible.

When Brother K finally paraded the five suspects in front of the school, I realized I could get away with it. I had the moral problem of seeing others being punished for my crime, but before Brother K even got a chance to start the punishment, some of the boys in our class got up the courage to protest and say it was a massive injustice. They began to accuse Brother K of acting outside natural law. It was Packer, above all people, who stood up and spoke out.

'It's not fair,' he said. 'You have no right to punish people without proof. It's morally wrong.'

Packer became the hero of the day, as if he had taken the instrument of torture himself. He had taken my place and was now going to be famous all over the school, like the leader of some great rebellion, full of courage and selfless inner strength. Others in the class began to back him up, as if he had given them the strength to speak out at last. He had liberated them. It was happening all over the world at the time. There were black civil rights marches in America. People protesting against the war in

Vietnam. Civil rights marches in Belfast and Derry too. We could see the trouble coming on TV, police punishing innocent people on the streets who were trying to run away. The British army bursting into people's houses. Things could not go on like that for ever.

Everybody was arguing openly now. Some of the boys were talking about the Geneva Convention. Others were talking about the final court of justice, quoting bits from *The Merchant of Venice* and *The Mayor of Casterbridge*. In the middle of all this, people jumped up and began shouting, saying it was a return to barbarism and lynch law. Summary judgment.

'It could have been anyone,' somebody said.

The whole class was on its feet. I jumped up as well and Brother K was suddenly overwhelmed by dissent.

'Maybe it was me,' I shouted, and they all thought it was the best joke ever, because I was the last person they imagined as the culprit.

'Yeah,' they started saying after me. 'I did it. It was me, brother.'

Brother K was finally forced to back down. He didn't give in easily and turned on Packer instead.

'Behold, the true culprit,' he said. 'Masquerading as a liberator.'

It was Brother K's only way out. He wanted to turn the rest of the class on Packer like wolves, hoping they would tear him apart. He suspended the punishment of the five suspects, hoping the class would take out its pre-emptive revenge on Packer instead. He resumed the classes and everything went back to normal. He was waiting patiently for the perpetrator to seek recognition for his crime. He was certain it would not be long before the real culprit would step forward into the light.

Nobody ever owned up and nobody ever guessed the truth. In the end, they all believed it was Packer who had done it, only that he still wouldn't admit to it openly. The more he denied it, the more they believed it was him, because they needed to solve this mystery and decided he was their revolutionary folk hero. He remained silent whenever they asked him, as if he was above praise. He had the integrity of a real leader, they said, the person who refused to take the glory for himself. Only the great people in this world have such an assured vision. He became untouchable and I think even Brother K began to respect Packer's inner strength and leadership.

I had the power of the real knowledge on my side. I carried the secret with me that could have shattered Packer's character in front of the whole school. I could have spoken up and declared him a fake. I could have said he was an impostor, a mountebank, a false hero living on the courage of his people. I could have reduced him to a tumbled statue from a forgotten empire, like Nelson. I could have told Brother K and all the schoolboys to follow me out onto the street, all the way into the Municipal Art Gallery next door, and pointed to the painting of the Dutch woman. There is your instrument of torture. But I didn't want that glory for myself. Instead, it became part of my secret life, part of the underground life that I lived in hiding. It was Packer who remained the hero, and even though he still refused to talk to me, it was a consolation to know that he needed me to keep this secret, even though he didn't know it. He was carrying the glory and I was invisible.

There was a lecture given by a great art historian in the gallery one day and we got the afternoon off to attend. He explained the origins of the Dutch movement of portrait painting. He called it the golden age of Dutch genre painting. He explained how they had an obsession with painting women writing letters or reading books. Everybody thought it was very boring altogether and there was only a snigger at one point when the art historian mentioned a famous painting called *Woman at Her Toilet*. He didn't have much to say about the Dutch woman with the gilded frame, except that it was interesting that there was so little furniture in the background. I was staring at the painting and everybody must have been wondering why I was so interested, as if I saw some hidden meaning in this Dutch portrait that no art expert had yet noticed.

I kept going back into the gallery on my own. I stood in front of the painting and thought about the instrument of torture hidden on top of the frame. I wished I could have told people and created a story of liberation around myself. I kept reminding myself of things that my mother told me and could never tell the world either, secrets that she kept in her diary, because that was her only real friend in life.

There was another painting I came across in the gallery, even more interesting than the Dutch woman. It was the beheading of John the Baptist. I knew it had something in common with my own story and the way I was unable to move on in time. John the Baptist was kneeling down at the centre of the painting with his eyes closed, his neck exposed, hands behind his back. To the right behind him, a soldier, dressed in flowing clothes, swinging the sword. It made me understand the power of an artist, the secrets they carry in their heads and the way they can slow a moment in life to a standstill. I could not stop thinking about the agonizing, endlessly revolving movement in this painting. The soldier's arms were full of strength and tension. You could see his muscles tight with action and the sword only two seconds away from slicing through the neck of John the Baptist. You could foresee the next moment clearly when his head would fall to the ground and roll away, while his decapitated body surged with a fountain of blood through the severed neck. You could stand there in front of the painting, waiting, hoping it would not happen, thinking somebody could say something and it could still be stopped at the last minute. You could stand there knowing exactly what was coming next, but the sword would never reach that point.

I looked at this picture like a big film on screen. I stood in front of it and thought of Sophie Scholl when she was sent under the guillotine in Munich. I thought of the trains going to Auschwitz. I thought of bombs stopped in mid-air over cities. I thought of guns pointing at heads. People waiting with hoods over their heads in police stations up North. That quiet moment in the street before a car bomb goes off, before the timing device changes everything beyond recognition. I thought of the Enola Gay in mid-air, like a stationary Air-Fix model in the sky over Japan. I was stuck in that revolving moment of history, paralysed and unable to move forward in time, unable to live in the aftermath and still wishing I could hold everything up like an artist. I was forever stuck in this pre-calamity, this pre-beheading, this pre-gas chamber moment when everything was fine, but already too late.

Then one day I heard that Packer was injured in a motorbike accident. He had broken his leg and was in hospital. Some of my class went to visit him and said he was having a great time with all the nurses laughing at his jokes. I started thinking of going to visit him myself, but I was afraid that he would not talk to me. It was my mother who encouraged me to go and see him. She knew that I had become invisible and told me to walk into the hospital and not care.

So that's how I walked into the ward and Packer seemed shocked at first when he saw me. He didn't know what to say. We shook hands and he smiled at me. Instead of talking about what happened between us, he started telling stories. He sat up in bed with his leg in plaster, with lots of signatures and little drawings on it, most of them made by girls. There was chocolate and fizzy drinks and flowers everywhere. He said he had been given morphine and it felt like he was rolling around in his bed like a marble, down onto the floor, into the steel bedside locker beside him with the door closing behind him. He never said a word about the fact that he had cut me off. We never spoke about that and just became friends again as before.

All that is over now and I have begun to pretend that nothing ever happened. Since then Packer has been trying to make up for the silence, including me in everything he does, getting me the job at the harbour. But something has changed, as if I can never fully trust friendship again after that. I can never tell him anything about myself and I have decided to remain in hiding. And maybe that's what friendship is, this uneasy pact between two different people, between the person who carries the glory and the person who carries the secret. It's as if he needs me now as much as I need him. It's the pact of heroes and followers, of pop stars and fans, of idols and admirers. It's the pact between the artist and the person he paints, the pact between the storyteller and the person who lives inside the story.

So now that's all in the past. It's Packer and me working together at the harbour, sitting in a boat, drifting away and looking up at the clouds, listening to the sound of hammering somewhere in the distance. We see Tyrone coming out of the harbour, bringing a group of models out to the island along with a photographer. We follow them at a distance and see them setting up on the island with Tyrone sitting in the background drinking a small bottle of whiskey. We watch them for a long time being photographed in their swimwear, changing behind a canvas screen and coming out in new costumes. One of them has to hold a basket full of mackerel. One of them wears a bathrobe, leaning back on the rocks, almost falling off the edge into the water and showing her legs. Another one in a leopard-skin swimsuit and a straw hat, chasing after the goats. Another picture of two girls together in miniskirts and high boots feeding seagulls.

When Tyrone arrives back in the harbour with the models, I can hear Dan Turley muttering and cursing because he's jealous that Tyrone got the job of bringing the models out to the island. Tyrone is younger and more handsome, and looks like the kind of man who hangs around models all the time, laughing and offering them cigarettes. Tyrone helping the models with their bags. Tyrone holding a model's hand and assisting her out of the boat, as if she's stepping out of her dress. Tyrone getting his picture taken with a big smile on his face and his arms around all the girls.

When the models come up the steps onto the quay, I hear one of them saying that she's covered in mackerel scales and feels like she's slept with a dead fish. They look pale and thin, as if they have not eaten in days. They put on some new lipstick and more perfume to cover up the smell of fish and petrol and seaweed all around the harbour. They try to look like they belong on solid ground again and have nothing to do with the sea, but they stumble on their high heels and have to hold on to each other as if their legs have been turned to jelly by the waves. Maybe they're not feeling very well after the journey back across the bay in the small boat. Packer tries to talk to them. He's not afraid of women and has things to ask them. He wants to know what magazine they're going to be in, but the models are not very friendly. They won't answer him and maybe they think boys shouldn't be so interested in women's fashion magazines.

One of the harbour boys then takes a dead mackerel from the fish box and holds it out in front of his groin. He starts walking around with the tail end of a mackerel wiggling out in front of him, showing his floppy mackerel mickie off to the world. The models look at him in disgust. They say we're a pack of little perverts. Gurriers. One of the models even gets sick over the side of the quay at the sight of the harbour boys running around with blue and silver mackerel mickies in their hands. Mackerel mickies with green stripes and black zigzag designs. Dangerous-looking mackerel mickies with rigor mortis. It's the first time I've ever seen Dan Turley grinning, because now we've all become run-alongs after him, making a big joke of Tyrone and his models. Mackerel mickie boys running around yelping and laughing, chasing each other around in circles until one of the models is forced to smile.

But then I notice that Packer has not joined in. He stands back with his arms folded, just watching. He wants nothing to do with this because it's all just vile and ordinary.

Twelve

All the news on radio and TV is about Northern Ireland and about Vietnam. There are lots of new words and phrases being invented, like sectarianism, direct rule, internment without trial. Meaningful dialogue, terrorist suspects, strip-searching, inhuman and degrading treatment. You could learn good English by listening to the news, because everybody is trying to find better ways of expressing what's going on and how they feel about things. They have to find new alternatives for words like evil and bloodshed and shock and horror, because the words often become meaningless. They come up with versions for things like containing the situation, weeding out individuals, descending into violence. There are new terms like arms caches, safe houses, plastic rounds, dawn raids, Nationalist concerns and Unionist positions. From Vietnam we are learning words like defoliation, infiltration, heavy pounding and carpet bombing. You can also learn geography and we have the echoes of exotic names in our heads, like the Ho Chi Minh trail, the Falls Road, Da Nang, Divis Street Flats, Portadown, the Tet Offensive and the Ardoyne. In Vietnam, they're using a substance called Agent Orange to get rid of all the forests where the enemy can hide, and in Northern Ireland they're leaving no stone unturned to root out the perpetrators. One day my mother found orange specks on the sheets hanging out on the line and was alarmed that Agent Orange could have started drifting that far across to Ireland on the clouds. She was afraid of war coming back again. But then my father examined the sheets when he came home and said it was nothing, only our own bees occasionally relieving themselves in the air as they flew out over the garden.

There are lots of other things happening as well. New things being invented, new food in the shops, like yoghurt. People were talking about a very fashionable new fruit called avocado. There's lots of new music on the radio by the Rolling Stones and Perry Como and Bob Dylan singing about 'No direction home'. Everything is moving forward into the future. Everybody loves air hostesses and nurses. There are new models of cars like the Commodore and the Cortina. And this summer, it's obvious that things are never going to be the same again in Ireland or anywhere else, because I saw a photo on the front cover of the *Irish Press* one day of a woman in a white miniskirt and white boots and a broad white hat, lifting her weekend case onto a train while a nun in a black habit was waiting patiently behind her.

Packer sometimes talks to me about how he's going to get a sports car. One of these days, he says, he will be driving a white, open-topped, two-seater. He's going to grow a moustache and speed about the place and get a twenty-foot boat so we can sail around together. He talks about what's going on in Northern Ireland and says his mother comes from up there and that she was once hit by the lash of a drumstick on the street when she was only nine years of age. She was standing by the railings, watching the Orange Parade going by, when one of the drummers lashed her right across her neck and she still has the scar.

On TV, we watch the Loyalist Protestants march through the streets on the twelfth of July, celebrating their most important day, the day that King Billy won the battle of the Boyne. They are called the Orange Order and they march through Catholic Nationalist areas of Belfast with Lambeg drums and flutes called fifes. My father makes a joke about them and says they're worse than Agent Orange and they could defoliate the entire rainforest with their noise. He worked up there for the British army, just after he qualified from university as an engineer, and says the sound is deafening. They use flexible drumsticks and some of them will play those things for twelve hours until their hands are bleeding with hatred. They beat those drums every year to ensure that nobody forgets about their history. It's the only way to keep your memory alive, that is to make as much noise as possible, my father says. The bigger the drum the less likely it is that people will forget.

My mother says it's the British Loyalists and the Irish Nationalists telling each other that they have a longer memory. She watches the marchers and cannot understand why there is so much trouble about it, with people rioting and setting buses on fire. She says it's not such a bad thing, men marching around with drums like massive bellies in front of them. But my father says she's making a big mistake, because the Lambeg drum is an instrument that is intended to offend Catholics and remind them that they don't belong in their own country.

'It's not that simple,' my father says. 'You can't always put Irish history through the German sieve. It's Loyalists marching against the Nationalists, just to antagonize them. It's people who refuse to be Irish making noise to drown out the people who want to be Irish.'

'Why don't they join in with them?' my mother asks.

My father smiles and it's clear that she's using German history to try and resolve what's happening in Ireland today. She is always making comparisons, saying that the Irish think with their hearts and the Germans think like the horses, only with their heads. She tries to stay positive and keeps asking why the Nationalists don't just get one or two drums of their own and join in. She thinks they are all children up there in different gangs and if they could only come together they would have a great time in one big band. My father tries to explain that the Nationalists have been kept down for years and that the Loyalists want everything for themselves. The drummers are the playground bullies who want to torment everyone else and remind them that they are the favourites with the British teachers.

'Why be offended?' my mother asks. 'You can only be offended if you want to be.'

'It's aggression,' my father says. 'Naked aggression, deliberately walking through Catholic areas to provoke them.'

My mother keeps trying and I like the new way that she has found to argue with my father, a kind of talented optimism that drives him mad. She thinks you can win people over by capitulating, by being so friendly that the aggressor has nothing to fight against. She always told us not to be interested in winning, never to strike back, never to become like the fist people. She says they should invite the Loyalists into their areas and tell them they are welcome to march down their streets and make as much noise as they like. They should invite them into their houses for cups of tea and make little cakes for them with hundreds and thousands on top, because sooner or later the kindness will spread and they will stop getting any fun out of provocation. They both want the same thing in the end, don't they, they both want peace. Who cares what flag you're waving? In fifty years' time, she says, they will all be marching together and it will be like one of those great street festivals they have in Rio de Janeiro, like the Fastnacht carnival in Germany, with people dancing all day and all night, and visitors coming from around the world to join in. It will be the festival of forgiveness, the festival of kindness winning over aggression.

My father shakes his head. 'It won't work,' he says. 'I've been up there. I've tried talking to them.'

He slaps his hand on his forehead and begins to make another speech. He says the Nationalists in Northern Ireland have tried everything. They tried capitulation, just like the Jewish people tried being soft and submissive in Germany and it didn't work there either. Now it's my father who starts putting Irish history through the German sieve. He always has to have the last word and says the Irish have to make their own noise. We have to make ourselves heard with our own language, our songs and poetry and stories, because that's the only way to stop yourself from being drowned out and becoming extinct. You have to keep staying alive in your own language.

Day by day, things are getting worse up there with car bombs going off in the streets. My mother finds it hard to understand why. She cuts out a picture from the newspaper of a wrecked street and puts it into the diary along with all the other nightmares. You could see buildings almost completely destroyed, the windows blown out, curtains hanging out and injured people being brought away. At night in black and white, under the flash of cameras, the blood looks black and the faces very pale. People look dazed and half asleep as they walk away with their hair full of white dust. My mother says she saw lots of things like this before with her own eyes and it reminds her of Germany during the bombing of the cities. She takes in a sharp breath and shakes her head.

'*Schon wieder*,' she says. 'Not again.'

She says it makes her sick. She saw this kind of thing during the war when she was bringing soup to Mainz. She knew the city when it was so beautiful. The next time she saw it she could hardly believe it was the same place. She kept losing her way. She said that some parts of the city just looked like open ground, with piles of rubble. Many of the buildings were cut down to half their size, with furniture and beds hidden underneath the debris. Some houses still had one or two walls left standing and you could see pictures hanging on their hooks and curtains untouched as if nothing had happened. She heard of people being killed by those falling walls, long after the bombing was over. You could see the horizon where a street had disappeared. Some of the houses left standing were black and burned out and still smoking. People were talking about phosphor as if it was some kind of disease that had spread across the city. They were saying that some of the people were not recognizable, they were so badly burned. People burned alive in the cellars like rags, holding on to each other, with cups and jugs lying beside them intact. One boy rescued his family from the inferno by breaking into a disused synagogue and finding a safe place in the baptismal font in the basement. The survivors hurried away out to the country with some of their most precious belongings on carts. Nobody knew who was alive and who had fled. People were crying everywhere and calling each other. People digging through the rubble for their relatives even days after the bombing, calling out names and listening for an answer, covered in white dust. There were signs left up in chalk handwriting to let people know where the occupants could be found. In one of the streets there was a mass funeral, with lots of bodies lying out in a line, and my mother says she could hardly make the sign of the cross. She says she saw her own hand coming up in front of her eyes, shaking so much that she felt like an old woman.

Every time a bomb goes off on the street in Northern Ireland, I can see the look of fear in my mother's eyes. My father too, because that's not his way of fighting for survival.

'It's what they called moral bombing during the war,' my father says. 'The IRA are taking lessons from Churchill and Truman. Bombing cities. Bombing the vulnerable people and the children.'

'It's all the same nightmare factory,' my mother says.

And then it's time to change the subject. Pointing the finger doesn't make you innocent, she says, as she takes out a German board game called '*Mensch ärgere dich nicht*' which means: 'Don't let it get to you, man.' It's raining outside. There is no point in going down to the harbour, so I agree to play chess with my father. My mother puts on a lamp. There is music playing on the radio. She even takes out the bottle of cognac and pours a small glass for her and for my father, because she wants everything to be without resentment. She brings out a box of chocolates hidden in the press in the front room and it's all chocolates and cognac smells and silence and Maria saying 'Oh no' when her luck runs out and she has to go back to the beginning. We're all great winners and losers and everybody keeps playing and concentrating. The only noise you can hear is the rain outside and the sound of Bríd as she keeps breathing up and down. My mother puts her arms around her and looks over at the chess board to see how things are going between me and my father.

'Whose move is it?' she asks.

'It's my move,' I tell her.

She admires the way we can play without speaking a word. My father taught me chess and I've only beaten him once, when he was still being polite, showing me my mistakes. For a long time we were courteous, warning each other about possible dangers. Mind your queen. Did you forget about your castle? It wasn't about winning but more about learning and enjoying the great moves you could make. My father never wanted to win against me and I didn't want to beat him either, so we kept avoiding the basic principle of chess. It was a kind of polite chess with no mean sneaky moves, no gambits. Now we've begun to take it seriously and don't say a word. Even long after the others have stopped playing their board game, my father and I are still sitting across from each other, taking ages for each move.

'Such concentration,' my mother says. She admires the way we can become so involved in the one thing and leave all other thoughts behind. It looks like she wants to distract us, because she offers the chocolates one last time, taking off the cardboard sheet to reveal another full layer underneath. 'Who would like a last chocolate, before they disappear?'

Everyone is looking at the box of chocolates and I pick out a toffee that is going to keep me going for a long time.

My father looks at the pictures of the sweets and the names of all the different shapes. He picks out a caramel delight and puts it into his mouth. He chews silently. I try to chew without any noise, but I have a struggle on my hands with the toffee which is like a big football in my mouth.

'It's still your move,' my father reminds me.

So then I concentrate as best I can. I glue the toffee up against the ceiling of my mouth, so that it's plastered like a gum-shield against the palate. I can't help sucking it, but at least I don't have to chew it any more and make swallowing noises that are very irritating when you're playing chess. My father is waiting and when I look at the board again, I make a quick decision. It's only afterwards that I realize what a brilliant move it is, a bit of chess genius.

My father is trapped. He's going to lose his queen. He stares at the board, trying every possible move in his head to get out of it. I keep the toffee-shield stuck to the roof of my mouth. The whole room is silent, waiting for the end when he shakes hands with me and says I'm getting better all the time. There is no way out for him. He's doomed. I imagine it from his side and check every possible move. I can feel a rush of excitement, knowing that I have beaten him at last. It's not polite either to boast about your move while he's still thinking, so I don't say a word until he eventually looks up at me. He has a fierce look in his eyes, blinking behind his glasses, and I cannot help smiling a little because the whole thing was just a fluke.

I want to help him. Maybe I should take back the move and allow him to protect himself a little better. He looks at the situation once more, but not for long. Then he puts his hand underneath the board and tips it over, before storming out of the room.

'What's going on now?' my mother asks.

She jumps up from the table. She wanted the evening to end on a good note. The chess pieces are rolling across the table. My sister Ita bends down to pick up the fallen black king from the floor, but my mother tells her to leave it there.

'Nobody is to touch anything.'

Everything is left there as it fell, with the chess board upside down and some of the pieces rocking back and forth, as if they were still alive and trying to get up to fight another day. My mother wants it all to stay like this, untouched, like a monument. My father had lost the ability to differentiate between a chess game and world events, as if everything is still a battle between black and white pieces. She goes up to the front room to tell him that chess is not war. She wants him to come back and not leave things as they are. She puts her arm around him, but he won't be moved.

The rest of us are left staring at the ruins of the game on the table for a long time, waiting. But then I decide to pick up the pieces myself. I want to make it easy for him to come back and set up the board again. I want to tell him we'll start a new game and this time I'll try not to be so mean and sneaky. The board is ready and I want him to come back, just to play and not think of winning or losing. I wait and listen to the rain, like the sound of wheels spinning outside the window. Dozens of them spinning and whirring on their axles without stopping. Wheelbarrows. Upturned bicycles freewheeling silently. Every wheel in the world rolling along the gutters and gurgling away into the drains. I wait and wait, but he doesn't come and we never again play chess after that.

It's my mother who comes back and tells me a story so that I will understand my father. She wants me to think of him as a small boy living with his mother and his younger brother Ted in the village of Leap. His mother sent him out to get milk one evening when the moon was already out. The blue dusty light was falling across the street and made the houses look like cardboard fronts. Everything looked unreal in this soft white light. He carried an enamel canteen up the road to the farm and watched the woman milking for a while. The cows were restless and he watched the tail slapping into the bucket. He heard the woman speaking to the cow as she filled the canteen with warm frothy milk. He didn't have to give her any money right away, because his mother always paid little bits off her bills in rotation. On the way home, the moon was so bright that my father fell and dropped the canteen of milk, because he was born with a limp and couldn't trust himself walking.

'The moon knocked me,' he cried, when he got home.

His mother rubbed his head and said there was no harm done. She cleaned the cut on his knee and said it was no use crying over it. She didn't want him to think it was the limp that was to blame, so she went to the door and spoke to the moon, pointing up into the night sky. Stop trying to trick people into thinking it's daytime. My father must have thought it was still his fault that there was no milk for the morning. And now he's still trying to make up for it and put things right long after they've happened and cannot be changed any more. He's repairing history, my mother says, trying to pick up the moonlight from the street.

Thirteen

There has been no news from Stefan. Weeks have gone by since he left our house and my mother is worried that he has not sent any more postcards. She received one card from a place called Kilfenora, saying thank you for all the small packages of barm brack which she had packed for him, but nothing after that. All she got was a letter from Tante Käthe, saying that she has heard nothing. They are very worried because Stefan is the kind of person who is brought up to be polite and keep in touch, but now something is preventing him from writing home.

I can't tell my mother about the conversation I had with Stefan, because she will be even more worried. I can't tell her how he wants to run away from his father and Kilfenora isn't even far enough away. I think of him in the West of Ireland somewhere finding another parcel of barm brack hidden in one of the secret side pockets of his rucksack. I know what that's like, because Franz and myself went on a cycling holiday together one summer, down to West Cork, and my mother packed our bags as if we were going to war and we might find ourselves in a place where there was nothing to eat.

At the dinner table she asks everybody to think hard and imagine where Stefan has gone to and why he hasn't been in touch, even if only to say that he's fine. He doesn't have to wait for something awful to happen before he contacts us. I can see that she is trying not to worry prematurely, but she feels responsible for any German visitor who comes to Ireland and gets lost. So we're all sitting around thinking of Stefan eating the last piece of barm brack somewhere, taking shelter from the wind and looking out over the Atlantic. Everybody is silently searching the cliffs and the beaches in their minds. I think of him trying to learn Irish so that he can disappear completely from view and become invisible like all the other Irish speakers in Ireland. I can see him pretending to be fully Irish, trying to get rid of every trace of his German accent, giving the woman in a bed and breakfast in Kilfenora a false name, and her saying to herself that he's a bit too tidy in his bedroom to be really Irish. I can see him moving across the mountains and the bogs, going into a pub and just nodding like everyone else and saying as little as possible, maybe telling people that he's from Northern Ireland, from Belfast, so they don't think his accent is strange. I can imagine the men in the pub saying that he looks a bit like the great German footballer, Beckenbauer, God bless him, and Stefan saying he wishes he was, but that he's got two left feet and one of them is facing backwards.

So the letters are starting to go back and forth to Germany and everybody is wondering why Stefan is not in touch. After more crisis meetings and phone calls from Tante Käthe, they finally decide to call the Gardai.

It's the first time that we've seen anyone in uniform in our house since I was very small, when there was a fox in the kitchen and the Garda came to tell us it was not a fox at all but a rat. This time it's two Gardai who arrive in a squad car. They are brought into the front room and even though my mother has asked them to sit down like any other guests, they remain standing at first. There is an older sergeant who is quite thin, and a younger, more heavy man making notes. Neighbours passing by on the street outside must be wondering what is going on, if somebody in our house has broken the law. My mother is afraid of policemen and immediately begins to talk, telling them lots of things about Stefan that are not really all that relevant, like the fact that he did very well at school and that he's got no reason for not returning to Germany to study medicine. She is disappointed that they are not taking more notes and begins to tell other things, looking for something that they will find worthy of putting down.

My father stands at the fireplace and says nothing for a while, then suddenly breaks in to condense a number of things my mother has been trying to say into a few neat words, like a synopsis. The Gardai keep looking at her and seem to think the whole thing has more to do with her, because she is German and they have come because of Stefan, a missing German tourist. My mother shows them the card which she got from Kilfenora and the sergeant passes it on to the younger officer who looks closely at the date on the postmark and takes a note of that.

The sergeant asks what Stefan's financial position was when he left our house and my mother says he must have run out of money by now, which is why they are so worried, because he hasn't written home looking for any money either. My father adds that he lived on very little in his student days, but nobody can live on what Stefan had. The sergeant then tells my mother to sit down as if it's his house and she is the guest. He explains that the Gardai will do their best to try and locate Stefan, but there is no reason to be alarmed at this early stage and they don't want to refer to him as a missing person as yet. The Gardai in the West would be keeping an eye out, he said, and in the meantime, it would be no harm to have a description. So then the Garda with the notepad sits down on a straight-backed chair in order to take down the details.

Everyone tries to remember what Stefan looks like and what he wore when he was leaving. My mother begins to say that Stefan is tall like his father. He's got a friendly face and brown eyes, like his mother. My father knows what the Gardai are looking for, so he begins to give them a detailed description of Stefan's rucksack, but then it is clear that he has never described anyone before in words like this and can't even remember the colour of Stefan's hair or jacket. They have to call Franz into the room, because he has the best memory in our house and can remember all kinds of dates and things that happened which everybody else wants to forget. He starts by saying that Stefan has thin legs and that he walks very fast, but the sergeant says he wants to confine it to appearances, so then Franz becomes nervous and can only remember that Stefan wore a grey jacket with a hood and blue jeans. The younger Garda says it's exactly what they were looking for and reads back the description.

'Tall, slim build, last seen wearing blue jeans and a grey, hooded anorak, carrying a green-and-white ruck-sack.' As we listen to these words, it sounds like Stefan will never come back. It's the description that nobody wants to hear, because it has taken all the life out of him and made him a missing person.

I'm not able to add anything except that Stefan has a mole on his back, but I know that is of no value to the police. All I can think of while the Gardai are in the house is that I am a criminal. I go through all the crimes I have committed. I listen to them in the hallway and imagine them leading me away to the squad car outside. I can already see the crowd of neighbours gathered on the street watching them drive away and me turning around in the back seat to take one more look at the house where I grew up. I have a recurring dream of this moment and imagine my mother at the door crying, saying she will bring me cake when I'm in prison.

When my mother talks about bringing people back to life, I know she is quietly thinking about Stefan. I think of Stefan out there in the West of Ireland, walking along the small roads in County Clare and Connemara, all the places I've been to, thinking that there is always something following him, like a shout in the air. He keeps walking and walking, but he will never get away from his own name, and his own family, and his own country. I think of him looking out at the sea, with nothing but the sound of the wind in his ears. And even though there is nobody around and he's picked the loneliest place in the world where there is nothing for miles, he can still feel that people are after him. I think of him looking out at the Atlantic as if he's been hunted like a rabbit and can't turn back. He's got no country to go back to.

The Gardai said they would leave it for another week. They told us that they would be keeping an eye out for him in the meantime, but we knew it would be impossible to find somebody who doesn't want to be found. We thought of him like the fugitive on the television series, always on the move to a new place. People in Ireland had disappeared to places like America and Canada, so they probably understood why somebody would not want to keep in touch. My mother sat in the front room a lot, thinking it was all her fault. She was wondering about all the things that might have happened to him, making up all kinds of accidents like falling off cliffs or breaking his leg on the side of a mountain and lying there starving and unable to pull himself down to the next village. She was starting the nightmare factory again.

And then I decided I had to tell her that Stefan was trying to be on his own. I wanted to put her mind at rest and told her he wanted to get away from Germany, from his father.

'He wants to disappear,' I said to her.

'What did you say?'

I could see how shocked she was to hear this. She wanted to know exactly what Stefan had said to me.

'You better be very clear about your answer,' she said, 'because this is a matter for the police at this stage.'

I was not sure what I was going to tell the Gardai when they asked me. It was out in the open now. I told her that Stefan said he felt numb in Germany and maybe she felt the same when she came to Ireland.

'He hasn't spoken to his father for a long time,' I told her.

'He told you that,' she said.

'Not for over a year,' I said. 'He wants to get as far away from his home as possible and disappear. He wants to go underground.'

My mother was silent for a moment. She was afraid of this German father-and-son war, because she must have heard it all from Tante Käthe. She said she knew there was trouble at home and now she was beginning to worry that Stefan was going to be a danger to himself out there around the Cliffs of Moher somewhere.

'He doesn't know the Irish landscape,' she said. 'It's not like the German mountains. Sometimes the wind comes up on those cliffs and picks people off like an invisible hand.'

She said she was constantly surprised by the wind in Ireland. After she got married to my father, he brought her on a honeymoon pilgrimage up to Croagh Patrick and she said she had to bend down and hold on to the rocks, otherwise the wind would have blown her down the mountain again. She was beginning to imagine the worst. She could not understand how Stefan could turn his back like that on his family, on the place where he grew up, on his own home.

'Will he not get homesick?' she wanted to know.

But that was exactly what Stefan was trying to be, homesick. He was trying to learn that feeling.

For a while the phone calls kept coming. My mother's school friend was thinking of coming over to try and set up a search party, but my father said Ireland was far too big a place to start looking for somebody who might not want to be found. My mother was in tears on the phone every day, because at times they thought Stefan was dead already. Onkel Ted came out to say a special Mass. They were only waiting for the day when his body would be found and I can see it in her eyes, how heartbroken Stefan's mother must be back at home in Germany.

At night our house is very quiet now, like a church where everyone is praying for him to return. Everybody is trying to remember him back to life again.

Then one day my mother was outraged, because she was on the phone to her friend and Käthe asked a question that seemed so thoughtless at this moment. She wanted to know if my mother had already given Stefan the ancient book from the time of Gutenberg. In other words, if Stefan was carrying the precious book with him. It seemed to my mother that Stefan's mother didn't even care about her own son as much as she cared about the valuable book, and if her son didn't come back, she hoped that at least the book would be returned. My mother could not understand her. She said it was no wonder Stefan had never learned to feel anything.

The Gardai had found no trace of Stefan and decided to make a public announcement. He was officially registered as missing and a message was broadcast after the news one day. We all sat around the breakfast room listening to the news in English until the message came at the very end, just before the weather.

'Here is a Garda announcement for Stefan Haas, a German national believed to be travelling in the West of Ireland. He is urgently asked to contact his family or any Garda station.'

It was great to hear that message being broadcast. I wished that I was Stefan myself. It was great to think of him hiding out there in the West of Ireland. I could imagine him hearing his own name being called out on the radio one day while he was sitting down to his dinner, maybe while passing by a public house with a radio on inside. I wanted to go missing like that and never come back. I could imagine him slipping away out of some town and the people looking after him, wondering if he was the German national they were all looking for. I could see him walking across the Burren, across the bogs of Connemara, trying to keep out of sight and moving further and further away from places where he might be spotted.

The Garda message was broadcast again a week later, but slightly altered this time.

'Here is a Garda announcement for a German national named Stefan Haas who is believed to be missing in the West of Ireland. He is of tall, slim build and was last seen wearing a grey jacket and blue jeans. Anyone who has seen him is asked to contact the nearest Garda station.'

Every time we listened to the announcement, I thought the description didn't fit him at all. It was not the way I remembered him. They should have said he looks like Beckenbauer, then everybody would have spotted him immediately. They should have asked if anyone had seen Beckenbauer hanging around the West somewhere, maybe checking into some bed and breakfast under an assumed name, pretending that he had no interest in soccer at all, only hill walking. They should have asked people to keep a look out for anyone kicking pebbles or maybe kicking an empty packet of cigarettes along the street. Maybe somebody saw him walking through the fields decapitating a thistle or a ragweed with the tip of his shoe.

Fourteen

Things were starting to escalate at the harbour, another word we picked up from Northern Ireland. One morning we came down to find that one of Dan Turley's boats had gone missing. He had already been out searching around the bay, but it was Packer and me who eventually found it out past the island and towed it back. It was badly damaged, lashed by the tide against the rocks, and had to be taken out of the water. The crane on the pier was brought into action and when the boat was finally turned over and placed on trellises for inspection, Packer said it looked like it had been mauled by a wild animal. There were scratch marks all over the bow and along the bottom. Here and there, the paintwork had been gouged and you could see the wet, sinewy wood, soft and yellow, like torn muscle underneath.

Dan Turley said it would take a lot of repairing before it could go back into the water. He was full of anger, as if this was all part of the plot to kill him off at the harbour. You could see the vulnerability in his eyes as he stared at the savage bite marks and ran his hand over the damaged areas as if the boat had endured great pain, as if it was one of his children. He patted the bow and said it would be alright once we repainted it with red lead, anti-fungus paint. Then he turned away with a hurt look in his face, wishing he could get the animal who did this, wishing he could break his bones like twigs with his big steel hands.

And then a few days later a second boat went missing. Dan was ready to kill somebody. Even though the harbour lads found the boat undamaged on the beach, Dan said he was being deliberately targeted. The people who were doing this were insiders who knew how to get to the moorings. They had to get to the lead boat first, which was tied from one pier to the other with long ropes, slack enough to allow the tide to go out. The ropes were often hidden underwater. Only a person with some knowledge of the harbour would have known how to get out to the other boats. The Gardai came to investigate and promised to keep an eye on the place, but Dan was not happy with that, and for two or three nights, he stayed hidden in his shed, sleeping on his bunk and listening to every sound outside. But there was no point in him being a watchman, he would have to stay there awake every night of the week, twenty-four hours a day.

The harbour lads were repeating Dan's words, saying they were going to crucify the man responsible. Nail him to the mast. Tie him to a lobster pot and sink the bastard. Already Dan had a fair idea who it was and stared around the harbour with great resentment, as if he would get his revenge some day soon. As he started fixing the damaged boat, his cursing increased.

Packer decided we were going to go on a trip to the West of Ireland. He told Dan we would be away for a week or two and Dan took this as a further conspiracy that we would suddenly abandon him in the middle of his crisis.

'Fecking off to the Aran Islands,' he growled.

I thought he might never want us to work for him again, but Packer was able to get around him, repeating the way that Dan said 'feckin' and 'running off' and 'Off on your travels, like a pack a' hooken gypsies.' At last the harbour boys started laughing again, and making light of the whole matter of the stolen boats as if it was just a freak event.

My father had nothing against me going to the Aran Islands. He was glad that I was going to a place where they still spoke Irish, but he didn't know that Packer was involved. I had my own money and maybe my father thought it was good that he could have the house to himself for a while, because I was like an enemy within.

Packer said it was going to be the first trip of many. We would travel all over Europe together, all around the world. He got a small gang of his best friends together from school and around the place where he lives, like an expedition to the Antarctic, with Packer as the leader and us as his crew, one with long hair and torn tennis shoes, another with glasses, carrying a coat with him every day, even when the sun was out. Another member of the expedition bounced along the street as he walked. Packer gave a running commentary on the trip, how we were going to discover the Aran Islands, how much beer we would drink, how many women we would meet, and how we were all characters in a big movie, Packer's expedition to the edge of the Western World.

The first thing we noticed going out to Aran was the light. It was coming from the opposite direction and felt strange. To us living in Dublin, on the east coast of Ireland, the world seemed to be turned around a full hundred and eighty degrees when we took the boat from Galway out to the islands. The white glimmer of sunlight that we expected to see when coming ashore was right there ahead of us on the way out to sea. It was like an inverted homecoming, something, Packer said, that was similar to getting on the plane in the autumn and landing somewhere on the far side of the world in spring. On the *Naomh Éanna* ferry out to Inishmore, it felt as though we were going backwards in time, travelling into the mirror. We were staring into the light over the Atlantic. We could barely see the shape of the three islands in the distance. We could smell the sea and the diesel fumes and feel the throb of the engines in everything we touched. We could hear the murmur of Irish being spoken around us on the boat and became aware, without saying it openly, that we were no longer facing east, towards London or Europe, but west, into an older, untouched world.

As we arrived on the pier in Kilronan, the afternoon sun was shining away towards the mainland. We walked up towards the American Bar which was like the island waiting room, where people looked out to see if the boat was coming in, where men spoke about the weather and decided whether the boat would go out again or whether you might be trapped on the island for another night. The people leaving the island were heading down towards the pier and the people arriving were filling their places at the American Bar. The tourists went straight out to the promontory fort at Dun Aengus, on foot, in pony and traps, or on rented bicycles. We were staying on the other side of the island at Killeany, so we made our way past the dance hall, past the low cliffs with the ivy, out along the road towards the small fishing harbour and the white strand which they call *trá na ladies* or the ladies' beach.

We explored the island over the next few days and

memorized the empty landscape around us. We saw the small Aran fields and the high stone walls, made of sharp grey limestone rocks, designed to let the wind through. We noticed how the tarred road was always fringed with a line of white sand and grass. We smelled the turf smoke and heard the sound of enamel buckets as we passed by the houses. Here and there a dog accompanied us part of the way and we realized how little traffic there was on this road and what a novelty we must have been, the strangers from Dublin. We saw the air strip in the distance with a single red fire engine parked in the middle and around twenty-five island donkeys roaming freely on the grass. We were told that every one of them had an owner, but they had the freedom of the island to come and go as they pleased, laughing at everyone as they went. We ran after them and trapped one or two of them, riding them like in a rodeo, falling off as soon as they bucked with their ears down. We went out to the Glasen rocks and the cliffs facing into the Atlantic, and saw nobody out there, only the balls of foam floating in from the sea and the booming sound of the waves smashing across the terraced rocks beneath us.

From time to time, I thought I would see Stefan out there on the cliffs, silently watching the sea. I thought he would be standing alone some distance away, at the very edge of the rock, looking down at the waves pounding into the caves, just staring as if he could never turn around again or go back to Germany.

On the way back from the cliffs, we saw the men working in the fields. Sometimes we saw women and children walking along the road and we noticed that they took the side of the road, close to the wall, while we walked in the middle. Mostly we saw nobody at all and it was only after some days that we understood how empty this landscape really was, how hard it must be to live here, away from the mainland, away from the shops and crowded streets. At night, it was so dark that you could see the stars very clearly, not only the main shapes like the Plough, but a whole lacy spray of white in between. It was so dark sometimes that we had to hold our arms out in front of us and grope at the stone walls to make sure we were still on the road.

In Tigh Fitz bar in Killeany, we heard the men speaking in Irish and telling great stories. We heard the story of how a plane once landed on the island during the First World War and how the cows and horses were all frightened because they were not used to the sound of engines and motorbikes. There was one horse driven mad for weeks, running crazy all over the island, day and night, with all the islanders trying to trap him and bring him back to his senses. When a young man with a rope tied around his waist finally crept up to put a harness on the horse in a moment of exhaustion, he went fully out of his mind and ran out into the waves on the beach at *trá na ladies*, taking the man with him.

We heard other stories of drowning and stories of the supernatural. That's my story, they would say. Not a word of a lie. We heard of the Hollywood director who came to Aran and found a brother and sister who were so handsome that he asked them to go back with him and spend the rest of their lives in the movies in America. When they were going away on the boat, waving at the people they were leaving behind on the pier at Kilronan, the brother suddenly changed his mind and jumped off to swim ashore again. He was rescued and pulled out of the water by his friends, while the sister stayed on board and went to America where she became a famous actress and they never laid eyes on each other again. Late at night, the men would start singing the old *sean nós* songs. 'The Rocks a Bawn' was like a hit single on the island and somebody had to sing it every night or nobody could go home. And the singer often needed to hold the hand of another living person while he sang, usually that of a stranger, winding it around like a barrel organ to keep the song coming.

We had studied *The Playboy of the Western World* at school, so we knew that a man would invent any story around himself in order to attract the admiration of a woman. A man would fabricate his own biography in order to get shelter and belonging, he would turn himself into anything and fit himself into any image required of him in order to be accepted. We knew that the inspiration for the play by John Millington Synge came from a story of a man who once came to the island saying he had killed his own father with a blow of a spade and was then hidden by the islanders in a hole out by Kilmurvy, while the police were searching high and low for him.

I wondered whether the people on the island would treat Stefan in the same way. If they had heard the Garda message going out on the radio, would they ignore it because they understood when a man wanted to go missing voluntarily? They knew full well, not by any description of his clothes or his appearance, but by the look in his eyes and the way he would spend his days staring at the Atlantic, that this was the German who didn't want to go back, the man who had murdered his own father. They would say nothing, even keep him hidden from the Gardai, because they liked being on the side of the person who was trying to disappear.

We knew that the play had caused a riot when it was first performed, because Irish people didn't like themselves to be portrayed in this way. They didn't like Synge for giving the Aran Islanders primitive instincts and immoral ways of speaking about themselves. It was the word 'shift' which caused all the trouble, a word used long ago for a woman's undergarments. We knew that the riot in the Abbey Theatre had angered Yeats and provoked him to say 'You have disgraced yourselves,' a phrase we often used against each other in class. And we knew that the word 'shift' had taken on an entirely different meaning. Now it meant getting off with, scoring, or being successful with a woman. Packer would never have used the word himself, because it was a country term which, he said, came from dancehall culture, where shifting a woman meant getting her from the inside to the outside. But we knew it meant much more and implied end results that went far beyond that, something that involved making up any amount of lies and stories. We also knew that the verb '*bréagadh*' in the Irish language had multiple meaning. It meant telling lies as well as courting or flirting.

We got talking to some of the Killeany girls at the dancehall. They accused us of trying to grow fur on our chins to pretend that we were men. They asked if they could touch our faces and said they had felt more hair on the back of a door. We met them along the road or outside their houses, but rarely in the pub which was mostly frequented by men and tourists. They invited us into their houses for tea and barm brack, and Packer would keep talking for us all, telling great stories and turning us into amazing heroes with very interesting lives.

One night in Tigh Fitz, Packer got talking to a Dutch

girl who was staying on the island for the summer. She had been in a motorbike accident and had a plaster cast around her leg, sitting on the bench in the pub with her painted toes sticking out the other end. Packer was able to tell her that he had also been in a motorbike accident and had his leg in plaster for months. She was so beautiful that everyone wanted to talk to her and tell her any amount of lies. They watched her painted toenails twiddling around and told jokes and stories. The old men wound her hand around as they sang songs, but it was Packer who finally got his arm around her and helped with her crutches to make sure she didn't fall over when she was leaving.

The following day, we all went walking up to an ancient church above Killeany. We climbed the hill beyond the cottages with the Dutch girl and Packer following some distance behind us. She was wearing a red tartan skirt which flapped in the wind every now and again. Sometimes Packer called one of us back to carry her across the rocks. At the monastic ruin of *Teampall Bheannáin*, the breeze frequently revealed the entire stump of plaster. We looked at the crumbling walls covered in yellow lichen and understood for a brief moment how ancient this place was. Everybody was mostly keeping an eye on the Dutch girl and watching how Packer was talking to her.

On the way back through Killeany that afternoon, we came walking by the cottages and saw hundreds of salted fish laid out along the walls to dry. Each one of the cottages had fishing implements outside, lobster pots, oars, and buoys. At the harbour, we saw some men and dogs sitting around on the small pier and I looked for a long time at them, comparing everything with our own harbour.

We carried on walking past the cottages with Packer and the Dutch girl in front of us. The crutches were clicking slowly along the road, making it sound like a hospital ward in the open air. Now and again she stopped to take the weight off her hands, hopping around for a moment on her good leg and falling into Packer with her arms around him, looking back at us with a big smile and brown eyes. At one of the cottages, there was an old woman leaning at the gate, looking out at the sea and watching the slow procession going past. She began talking to us in Irish, first of all saying it was a fine day to be walking and doing nothing. She wanted to know where the girl was from and what happened to her leg. I explained that she had broken her leg in a motorbike accident and that she was staying on the island until the leg healed, before she went back to Amsterdam. The old woman began to laugh, saying there was not much to do on the island for a young woman with a plaster on her leg.

By now Packer and the Dutch girl had already moved ahead along the road, while we were still listening to the old woman and answering her provocative questions with shrugs and smiles. She asked us why we had no girlfriends and what was wrong with all the island girls walking up and down the road, day and night, with no crutches.

The old woman smiled. She was looking at us with humorous idleness, leaning lazily with her elbow on the wall. We could see the ancient teeth left over in her mouth and the deep lines across her face. We could see the marks of the weather and the wind and the rain around her sunken cheeks, but underneath, she had the expression of a young Killeany girl. Nothing could hide the mischief in her eyes as she watched us drifting away, calling out a final exhortation in Irish behind us.

'*Scaoil amach an deabhailín*,' she said with a wink. Let out the little divileen.

It took us a while to work out what exactly she meant. We began to understand why we felt the world had been turned around for us. It was not just the direction of the sunlight. We had been misinformed by the landscape and all its lonely features, because all the things we had expected to come from London, from Europe, were found here on the Aran Islands in great plenty.

'Let out the little *deabhailín*,' Packer kept saying on the train home as if we were going to follow the old woman's advice for the rest of our lives. It was his new phrase, the Irish for shift. He was the leader of the great expedition and he repeated the words like a souvenir all the way back to Dublin.

When we got down to the harbour again, everything in the world was turned back around, a hundred and eighty degrees. Dan Turley was full of muttering rage, not only at us abandoning him, but at the fact that another boat had gone missing and this time not even been recovered. Dan had to get somebody to drive him down the coast, checking in all the different harbours halfway to Wexford, without finding anything.

'I know who it is,' he kept repeating. 'I know the bastard.'

Dan said it was always his boats that were missing, not Tyrone's. And that said everything. By now the harbour boys had turned the place into a courtroom. They looked at everyone with suspicion, just like Dan, saying things about them that they had heard from other people. They collected gossip, lots of things that had nothing to do with missing boats at all. They were like the harbour conscience, like a jury muttering through the side of their mouths. They saw the schoolteacher and said she was having it off with the trawler man. They noticed his van parked outside her house, and how it meant her husband was away on business. They knew a man from the hill who came down to the harbour and said he was looking for planning permission to build apartments along the top of the cliff behind the harbour. How much did he have to pay in bribes in order to clutter up the most scenic place along the coast with ugly apartments, they kept whispering. Every new car, every wedding, every death, every accident and every drunk driving charge was discussed at the harbour.

Packer said we were going to help Dan to find the person who was stealing the boats. His idea was that we would stay out all night and keep a kind of vigil at the harbour. The harbour vigilantes, he called us, without telling the rest of the harbour lads or even Dan.

I had to sneak out the bedroom window after everyone had gone to sleep and cross over the roof with the bee-hives, down onto the wall and away around the back lane. My mother told me to put a schoolbag and extra pillows into my bed to make it look like I was asleep. She was helping me escape. At the harbour, I could not see Packer anywhere at first and he only stepped out from the shadow beside Dan's shed when I started calling him in a whisper. He had already decided where we were going to hide. He said we would sit in one of the boats, the best place to stay unnoticed. They would never accuse us of stealing the boats because we had been away in the Aran Islands.

We got out to one of the boats and settled down. He had two cans of beer and I had brought sandwiches that my mother made. Packer was annoyed when he realized that my mother knew about me staying out all night.

'Jesus. I don't believe it,' he said.

But I told him it was alright, my mother knew how to keep a secret. And she wasn't told about the whole vigilante idea. In any case, we were just sitting in the boat for hours, not doing anything against the law, just whispering. Packer was talking about the Dutch girl, saying he had got a letter from her asking him to come and visit her in Amsterdam. Then we listened to the sound of the water underneath the boats, and some of the masts clanging. The boats were moving back and forth, shifting around us like cattle in a barn. At one point, we saw the patrol car passing on the road, slowing down for a moment before it went out of sight around by the castle. But we didn't care that nobody came, because we liked being out at night when everyone else was asleep.

And then we saw somebody walking towards the harbour, a man brightening up and falling into shadow again as he passed under the street lights on the pier.

'Hark,' Packer said, and I started laughing.

Packer punched my shoulder to keep me quiet. We put our heads down to stay out of sight. The pier was behind me, so I left it to Packer to put his head up every now and again to see who it was, if we could recognize him. The man stood behind the upturned boat that was still being painted. He stood behind the crane for a moment, then moved forward to the edge of the pier.

'It's Tyrone,' Packer whispered.

We had got our man. I could already see us talking to Dan and talking to the Gardai. I could imagine them taking Tyrone away for questioning.

'He's coming,' Packer said.

We watched Tyrone bending down to untie the ropes

on the pier, then pulling the boat in and going down the steps. We saw him getting into the boat, his own boat. He was standing up and he stopped for a moment to pull a bottle out of his pocket and drink from it, before he picked up the oar and began to scull his way along the pier. He was coming right towards us. I thought he knew that we were there all the time and that he was quietly coming to get us, that he would hit us with the oar or shout to let us know he was no fool and he knew what we were up to. For one moment, he was right beside us, standing up, talking to himself, humming.

At the harbour mouth, he sat down and took out the second oar, then started rowing out slowly without a sound. He was so skilled at dipping the oars into the water each time, that they made no more noise than the water lapping against the granite steps. We had put him on trial. He was doing nothing other than taking out his own boat, slipping quietly out of the harbour, but we had already found him guilty.

'Let out the fuckin' *deabhailín*,' Packer whispered.

And then we started laughing so much that we could not even move. I had to put my head down on the seat of the boat because I was shaking so much and laughing without a sound. Packer repeated the phrase once more and we started laughing even faster than before. When we got back in to the pier, we were walking crooked and stopping every now and again to let out the laughter that was trapped inside us. We walked up onto the promontory field, above the harbour where they were planning to build the luxury apartments. For now we had the place to ourselves and sat looking out over the bay from up high. We could see Tyrone out there in his boat, with his back to the bow. He had tied up to the buoy of a lobster train, drinking from his bottle and smoking his cigarette. We could hear him starting to sing. He was sitting with his feet up on one of the seats, singing like an innocent man.

Fifteen

I know I will be judged by what the Germans did.

When my mother's job as a governess came to an end in Wiesbaden, when the American lieutenant and his family moved back to Vermont, they promised to find her a job with the American forces in Germany. She had spoken to them about wanting to become a chemist or studying law, so they found her a job as a court clerk in the denazification courts. Everyone in Germany had to prove their innocence after the war and the courts were set up to make sure that no Nazis would get back into powerful positions. Everybody had to fill in forms called 'Fragebogen' to state what they had done during the war years and whether they had belonged to the NSDAP. My mother had a clean sheet, except for one box which said she had joined the BDM, Hitler Youth for girls, but that was because she had no choice and she always told us she used the 'silent negative', as they called it in her family, withholding their allegiance to the Führer by expressing a silent resistance inside their heads. Her new job was to take notes of what was said in court and to type it up afterwards. She got a clothing allowance, a fine salary and an apartment all to herself, which was an unimaginable luxury at that time, she says. She had access to as much food as she wanted so that it was no longer a problem sharing it around Mainz and Rüsselsheim.

After the war, people in many key positions had to go before a tribunal to demonstrate that they had not acted improperly during the Nazi years. Before they were allowed to take up their old jobs as theatre directors, hospital consultants or university professors, many of them were forced to make a case before the tribunal and my mother says she witnessed grown men break down in the court when they were told they could not work because of their Nazi past. She saw a bakery manager who had continued to run the bakery after his Jewish employers had been thrown out and who was then thrown out of work himself after the war, even though he had nothing to do with the changes and claimed he only made 'Brötchen' all his life. There were some people who still believed in the Nazis and other people who didn't care very much one way or the other who was in power. There were lots of people who claimed they had just joined the party because they had to. My mother says it was usually the people who claimed they were innocent who were the most convinced Nazis and the people who acknowledged their guilt who were actually most innocent.

The small courtroom held about fifty people at the most, she told me. The person on trial was normally accompanied by his relatives, because they were all affected by the outcome. My mother had never been inside a courtroom in her life before and it was just as she had imagined, with a few rows of benches for onlookers and other benches for the prosecutor and the judge. The people before this court had no lawyers and usually defended themselves. The tribunal was led by an American officer, but my mother says she was actually working for a German prosecutor named Willenberger, who conducted each case. My mother says Willenberger was a very clever man who kept the most interesting piece of evidence until the very end, when the person before the court was already convinced of their innocence, then he would drop the most devastating fact, something that would make the accused and his relatives turn white with shock. And then she told me how when a person got the all clear, you could see the family members embracing each other outside the court afterwards.

Mostly it was only people who had obvious connections with the Nazis who were charged in the first place. You could see the hatred and resentment seeping through their statements, because they had been in control and now they were powerless. But sometimes there were marginal cases where it was hard to distinguish between being German and being a Nazi. Sometimes the difficulty for the tribunal was to choose between patriotism and Nazism.

One day, my mother says, a well-known gynaecologist was brought before the tribunal to answer for his attitudes during the Hitler years. She cannot remember his name now, but he had been in charge of a delivery unit at a hospital in Frankfurt and was accused of being anti-Semitic. He was a very quiet man who hardly tried to defend himself at all, only answering each question very briefly and factually. He said he had never used his position against anyone. He said he was forced to join the NSDAP and now he was forced to renounce the party, when in fact he had no interest in anything at all but delivering babies.

The prosecutor accused him of working directly for the Nazis, because every baby born in the Third Reich was a gift for Hitler. The gynaecologist then said children were not born Nazis. The arguments went back and forward for days with the prosecutor saying that he delivered only Nazi babies and the gynaecologist saying he didn't care what kind of babies he delivered as long as they were healthy. It was clear to my mother, who had to type everything up, that the arguments were going around in circles. Everybody was waiting for the final trick from the prosecutor, but this time it was the gynaecologist who waited until the last minute before bringing in his key witness. A Jewish woman had travelled all the way back from London to testify that she had had a baby boy while she was being treated by the gynaecologist. She said he knew the baby was Jewish, but had kept it secret.

The prosecutor argued that he had heard from other patients that he was an angry man, but the Jewish woman said he was always friendly to her.

My mother says it was very similar to the famous case of Wilhelm Furtwängler, the famous conductor of the Berlin Philharmonic Orchestra who stayed in Germany and continued to conduct all through the Hitler years. For the Nazis, he was the great showcase for German music, but Furtwängler himself said he was only devoted to the music. But music was not neutral, my mother says, no more than babies were neutral, because everything became part of the war machine. When it became law that no Jewish people could take part in German culture, Furtwängler refused and stood up for his Jewish colleagues in the orchestra, sending letters to Goebbels personally to protect them and keep them working with him. Because Furtwängler was such a famous conductor, the Nazis went along with him for a while. But as time went by and the Nazis became stronger, he found himself having to conduct under the Swastika, with Goebbels and other leading Nazi figures in the audience. There is a well-known moment after one of those concerts when Goebbels came to shake his hand. Immediately afterwards, Furtwängler took out his handkerchief to wipe his hand. Maybe it was a true sign of how he felt about the Nazis and their concentration camps, or maybe it was simply a sign that he had sweaty hands after the performance. It made no difference because the great German conductor had compromised his music, just as the great gynaecologist had compromised his profession, even though there were a lot of good babies born during the Nazi times. My father says there is a recording he would love to hear of Beethoven's Ninth Symphony which was made during the war with the sound of bombs falling in the background and it goes to show that Furtwängler was not afraid to die for his music.

The trouble at the denazification court began when my mother had to type up the reports and the prosecutor asked her to change things. He said she had mistaken some of the testimony and that what the Jewish woman had actually said was that the gynaecologist was always angry and hostile towards her. My mother was to put down that the Jewish woman was in fear of her life that the gynaecologist might suspect that she was Jewish.

My mother refused to write any of that. She said she had taken very careful notes, they could check her handwriting. The prosecutor then said she could lose her job if she did not comply, he would accuse her of trying to help a former Nazi. When she continued to refuse, he asked her if she was taking bribes from people. It was only then that she realized what was happening. She had seen packets of cigarettes and other things like cognac and tins of meat in the prosecutor's office at various times, so she began to understand why some people got the authorization to work and others didn't.

She decided not to work under these conditions any longer. She handed in a letter of resignation, stating that she could not go along with it. The letter caused an instant crisis. Before she had time to clear her desk and leave the office, the prosecutor, Willenberger, asked her to withdraw the letter. He said he would make it easy for her, all she had to say was that she had made a mistake and he would allow the gynaecologist to have his name put forward for authorization. Then he changed his mind and said he would bring her before the court herself and say that she had been friendly with the gynaecologist, that they had been seen together. He would see to it that she would be blacklisted.

My mother says she didn't need to make life so difficult for herself all the time, but she could not get the gynaecologist out of her mind, the way he sat there quietly without getting angry. The letter of resignation came to the attention of the American administrators who were responsible for the denazification courts, so they came and asked my mother if she had written this letter freely, without any pressure from anyone. They asked her if she wanted to take the letter back. My mother explained why she had come to this decision and says she felt very stupid, sitting there with a number of officers smoking and offering her cigarettes, asking her why she was so eager to give up such a good job. They couldn't believe anyone had a conscience in Germany and wanted to find out what was really behind the letter. It was only after a few days, when they realized that she was not going to change her mind, that they began to believe her.

The problem was that the letter was on file now. They must have thought she would contact the lieutenant from Vermont and tell him what had happened, so they were forced to take the letter seriously. They made more attempts to change her mind. The prosecutor asked her if there was anything she needed, things he could provide for her and her family. He even mentioned the use of a car. He was kind one minute and then turned aggressive. She was afraid and decided to leave immediately.

She thought she was safe back in Kempen, but the prosecutor, Willenberger, came after her, appearing on her doorstep, begging her to withdraw the letter. She could only assume that he had now lost his job as a result. It was going to be on her conscience that Willenberger was blacklisted. He explained that he had a wife and family and that she was making them all destitute with her grand, untouchable conscience. And what did she do during the Nazi years, why was she suddenly so worried about her conscience when she could live through the whole of the Third Reich and not ever have to write a letter like that before?

My mother says she wishes she could have had the courage to write that letter during the Nazi times, that she might have been more like Sophie Scholl and protested openly. But then she would not be alive now. And now is the time to reshape your conscience, she says. Maybe it was the silent negative that she and her family had kept in their heads that was finding its expression at last in words. At some point you stop being silent. She says it's even more difficult to resist now than it ever was under the Nazis, because there is more to lose. It's easier than ever to say it doesn't really matter all that much now. Just getting rid of every Swastika in the world is never going to be enough. Just because the Nazis are gone, doesn't mean that injustice is gone.

She would not change her mind. Willenberger kept following her around the town and people in Kempen must have thought he was a former fiancé whom she didn't want to marry any more. He sat behind her in church. He whispered that she had made him desperate and that if she didn't change her mind, he would do something really drastic, something she would not like to be responsible for. He even pulled out an envelope and said he could let her have a nice little sum of money.

'You cannot sting me,' she said aloud outside the church.

She could see the anger in his eyes and thought he was about to attack her. She says a woman knows when her life is in danger because you can smell dead leaves in the air and you can feel your legs going weak and lose all the colour in your face. She thought she had already met her killer. Very often when they found a woman's body, they first assumed she was a prostitute. It was something that Willenberger said to her then, that convinced her that he had been the true Nazi himself all along.

'You would not have lasted long,' he said. She took a few steps back. She was afraid to turn around and stood there until he finally left.

By this time, my mother had already applied for a visa to Ireland. She wanted to get as far away as possible. She was afraid to stay in her home town any longer. She didn't want to tell her sisters or her aunt any of these threats. Onkel Gerd knew and made sure she was always accompanied when going out. The weeks that she had to wait were agonizing. But then the visa came at last and the house was full of excitement. Even when she was leaving on the train and had embraced her family, even when she was still sitting on the train, wiping her tears, she knew she had still not got away, because Willenberger came after her.

My mother says she had never been so afraid in her life, seeing him smile from behind his newspaper. But there comes a moment, she says, when you have been so afraid for such a long time, that you don't care any more. Suddenly you become light-headed with courage. The train was full with people going into Krefeld and Düsseldorf, so she just suddenly spoke up to the whole carriage.

'I want you to leave me in peace,' she said in a raised voice. Everybody in the carriage looked around and stared at Willenberger sitting opposite her, until he eventually had to move away.

Sometimes my mother still thinks he will come after her in Dublin, that he will suddenly knock on the door. For years she had nightmares about men outside the house, sitting in a car, waiting for her to come out with her children. She had escaped to Ireland without losing her conscience. And then she laughs and says she would have made a terrible lawyer.

When she first arrived in Ireland, she felt so free. She vowed to go on her pilgrimage to Lough Derg. She had a job as a governess and was collected in Shannon by Mister and Missis Bradley who owned a public house and a shop on the main street in Ballymahon, in the middle of Ireland. They had three boys. She remembers the welcome that Mister Bradley gave her at the airport, clasping her hand with both of his, then taking her suitcase from her. They brought her to the car and made her sit in the front seat, so that she would see as much as possible along the journey. My mother thought they would go straight to Ballymahon and she was anxious to start working right away, but that was not how the Irish did things, she says, and the Bradleys first brought her to Ennis, where they stayed in a hotel and had a party. Mister Bradley knew lots of people in Ennis and invited them all to come for a drink. She says she could not understand why the Irish wanted to celebrate before she had even done any work. It was a poor country, a country that had not been bombed during the war but looked much more destroyed and starving than Germany. The party lasted until late in the evening with people toasting her and singing songs and a priest explaining the rules of hurling to her, even though she didn't understand how you could play with sticks and not hurt each other, so the priest told her that hurling was a substitute for war, like all sport and singing.

In Ballymahon, everybody in the town was talking about her and coming up to have a look for themselves as if they had never seen clothes like hers before, only in the films. Groups of children came to the public house to see her coming out and when she smiled at them, they were shy and held on to each other. She felt like a famous visitor. She was invited to dinner every evening, unlike the other people working in the pub and around the house. The Bradleys had made a lot of money during the war when Mister Bradley stored gallons of whiskey and boxes of tea which had become scarce. He had made so much profit selling these during the rationing, that even the Bank of Ireland came to borrow money from him because they were broke. But it wasn't long before my mother learned what Ireland was really like and why there was so much poverty that could not be explained by bombs.

Next door there was a small cottage where the door was always open. The little Bradley boys would run past and shout 'Dirty, Dirty.' She told them to stop, but they would not listen to her. It made no difference, they kept on shouting 'Dirty, Dirty.'

My mother went to the door of the cottage and looked inside. It was dark and smoky because of the small windows. It was true that the place was dirty. She couldn't believe that humans could live like this. There was not a single piece of furniture in the house, not even a chair, and the man sat on the earth floor beside the fire with his wife. My mother says his naked legs could be seen coming out under his ragged trousers like a skeleton. They never seemed to come out of the house. They must have been ashamed to be seen in the town and never moved from the spot where they were sitting.

My mother spoke to the Bradleys and told them what was happening. Mister Bradley laughed. Missis Bradley said the tailor and his wife were dirty people, living in squalor. My mother was not able to persuade them to control the boys, so she tried something else. The next time they shouted 'dirty' in the door, she decided to go in and apologize for them. She stepped inside the cottage and got the smell of poverty coming up from the two old people. She apologized for the children's behaviour and said she hoped they were not offended. The old people looked up and said nothing, because they didn't understand English. They could only speak Irish and the Bradley boys started laughing. Even Mister and Missis Bradley found it funny and my mother says the whole town was laughing at the idea of a German woman trying to apologize to the poor tailor and his wife when they only spoke Irish.

My mother then learned her first words so that she could go into the house and greet them in their own language. She found out their names as they were known to other Irish speakers around the town. *Páraic Mháirtín* and *Sinéad gan cainte.* The tailor even got up from the ground to come to the door and shake her hand. She says it felt like a thin black leather glove. It was soft and bony, with no weight at all left in it, and hardly any warmth. She can never forget shaking hands with somebody so poor and so destitute, but still so much alive.

She started taking some spare food from the house and bringing it to the cottage and the tailor thanked her in Irish. Missis Bradley didn't like the food going out of the house, but she didn't say anything except that she wanted her children to grow up clean. Everybody was afraid of being like the tailor and she wanted my mother to give the boys a few words of German instead of Irish.

She continued to bring food to the cottage from time to time under her coat, like she did in Germany. But unlike the Americans in Wiesbaden, the Bradleys got annoyed because my mother went too far. One day she asked if she could give away an old coat belonging to Mister Bradley. They were throwing it out onto the rubbish tip to be burned, an old brown torn coat which she cleaned up. She sewed on new buttons and fixed the sleeves, then brought it over to the tailor. After a few days, Mister Bradley came into the house in a rage, saying that he could not understand the Germans any more, because he walked along the street and saw the dirty, filthy Gaelic tailor standing at the door of his little cottage wearing his old coat. He was shocked to see what he would look like if he hadn't made all that money selling whiskey and tea. Missis Bradley said it was an outrage and that people in the town would mistake the tailor for her husband. After that, my mother decided it was best to leave her work with that family and moved to Dublin, where she met my father. But even when Missis Bradley brought her to the bus to say goodbye, my mother noticed that maybe she had begun to change a tiny bit, because she said my mother had done something that nobody else in the town was able to get away with. She wished her good luck and said she would be missed.

My father puts his arm around my mother and praises the way she stood up for the Irish language, for the people dying out and going into extinction. He says the Irish people began to pretend they didn't belong to the same country as the tailor and his wife. They made a foreign language out of their own tongue and that allowed them to become racist against their own people. He smiles and says my mother shook hands with a dead language and brought it back to life again.

Sixteen

I know I will be judged by what the Irish did.

When my father was studying engineering in Dublin and all the students were sitting in a lecture room in UCD waiting for the professor one day, there was an argument about Britain and Ireland, about Irish soldiers fighting for the Queen, about flags and languages, about a United Ireland and about Irish neutrality. Everybody was throwing everything they had into the debate and speaking at the same time. Some of them had their feet up on the desks, smoking cigarettes and saying it was a waste of time speaking about anything other than women and whiskey and emigration. My father called them cowards. He was good at mathematics and able to think sideways, so he took them all on and kept them silent for a moment with his ideas.

He told the other students that the Irish had to stop running away and start thinking with their heads in future. Some of them agreed and said the only thing holding Ireland back was the situation in the North of Ireland and the fact that the post-boxes were still red up there. Some said it could only be solved with blood. Others said it was pointless and that the heroes of 1916 died for nothing, just to change the colour of the post-boxes in the south to green. The students with their feet up said the problem was that Irish women never took off their clothes until they were married. And then came the big storm in the lecture room, when somebody made a remark about women wearing black shawls over their heads in Ireland and how that was what kept the Irish going backwards when all the women in England and France were now wearing headscarves and stockings instead.

Everybody laughed except my father. His mother, Mary Francis, wore a shawl. She was photographed in her shawl along with two other women also wearing shawls on the street in Leap, West Cork, by the famous photographer, Father Browne. My father got up very suddenly from where he was sitting. He picked up the steel chair and flung it across the room. He didn't tell anyone why he had decided to do this and they didn't know what secret thing in his head made him so mad. They must have thought the chair had conducted a massive charge of electrical energy, like a Van de Graaff generator underneath him. My father must have been surprised himself by the amount of noise the chair made clattering across the wooden floor. I don't know where he got the idea from, but he picked up another chair and threatened to kill everyone with it. The students took their feet down off the desks and fled with their backs up against the window, begging for mercy.

My father stood there with a wild look in his eyes. I've seen it many times myself when his eyes are like hard brown full-stops inside his round glasses, when his mouth is tight with rage and his ears are on fire. He's small and has a limp, but he gets so serious and so angry at the sound of his own words that everybody is afraid of what he might do. The students knew that he could be overpowered easily and that he was not very good at fighting, even with a chair in his hands. But he was good at losing his temper and not telling anyone why. So they began to talk to him and to ask him what it was that made him so furious. They were dumbfounded to find out that it was the Irish shawl and not something much more important like asking Britain for war reparations or keeping Irish people at home and stopping them from emigrating and working for Britain. They said there was no offence intended to him or to anyone in Ireland who still wore shawls, and slowly my father let the chair down again and everybody shook hands. Somebody picked up the chair lying on the floor, and after that, they were careful because they said my father was sensitive and had a short fuse and could lose his temper at the drop of a hat.

I didn't know about any of this at the time when I picked up a chair one day and threw it at my mother. There was an argument in the kitchen one morning about going out without clearing the table and I got angry with her. I couldn't get her to agree with me, so I picked up a chair to kill her. I didn't really want to hurt her, just to frighten her. She said she had been frightened by worse things than chairs, so I threw it across the floor of the kitchen. She didn't pick it up or say much, except that flying chairs would never make her change her mind, no more than flying words would ever persuade anyone to agree with me. She said she would leave the chair where it landed. For ever. It was going to be like a monument to the uselessness of anger. Everybody passing by would know by the chair lying on its side that somebody had failed to convince the world. The flying chair of lost arguments, she called it. So I picked it up again. We shook hands and it was all over. But I realized that I had become like my father inside. He invented the idea of picking up chairs because people were not listening, and the only thing that would make them take notice was the sight of something unusual, like a chair upside down in the air with nobody sitting on it. I could no longer avoid being like my father, no more than Stefan can avoid being his. I am a chair-thrower for Ireland and I wonder what I will do next.

Maybe it's a kind of father-and-son trap. No matter how much I try to be the opposite, I will still end up like my father. It's how evolution works, with every son slipping into his father's shoes, no matter how different your clothes are or how long your hair is or how different the music is you're listening to. All my friends will go like their fathers even if they don't go bald or wear glasses, because fathers and sons are not a line of separate individuals, as far as I can see. It's more like a chain of unfinished people, with each son improving things or making things even worse. A long line of fathers and sons heading into the future, all the way into infinity. Sons going backwards and sons going forwards and sons that are no better and no worse than their own fathers. I know we will be held accountable, not for what we do ourselves, but for what happened in the time of our parents, because it takes that long before people can look back to see what really went on and turn it into history. We are the ones who go on trial for what the people before us did.

One day, my father and his friends invaded Northern Ireland. Before he was married, he was politically active and belonged to a party which decided to invade the six counties which were still under British Rule. The leader of the party was Gearóid, a great friend who must have been like Packer for me, somebody who was able to make up a story for everyone around him, making speeches and inventing the future. It was a cultural movement that would reawaken the Irish people. The Irish language would give the people back their strength and courage. The Irish language is what would stop people going hungry and emigrating to America.

I sometimes think about the way my mother and father must have been on trains at the same time. I can't help thinking of them before they ever met each other, on trains going in very different directions, in different countries. My father sitting on a train to Belfast with his friends and my mother sitting alone on a train to Mainz. Him going up to persuade the people of Northern Ireland who wanted to remain with Britain, that they were making a big mistake. Her on the way to a city that was destroyed by the bombing. Him going to the city where the bombs were now starting to go off and her going to a city where there was not much more left to be destroyed. It's funny to think of them not knowing each other at all. Funny to think of a time when they would have walked past each other in the street and not even looked at each other, because they were both thinking only of the things they had to do for their country. Germany and Ireland were so far away from each other at that time. But they come together inside my head. They are not separate countries any more, because my father and mother got married and I have mixed up Irish history and German history so much that it's all the same place now.

When they invaded the North, my father was wearing a dark suit and a white shirt and tie. He wore a loose tweed cap that seemed a little too big for him and made him look like a boy. He had a tweed coat over the side of his arm and he was walking with a group of people, smiling and talking, following behind Gearóid. He was the head of the movement called Aiseirí and they were all getting on the train in Dublin, going to Belfast. You can see them in colour because there was a man travelling with them all the way who was making a film of the whole thing. They sometimes smile towards the camera, but mostly they walk with great determination and seriousness, because there's no turning back and they know exactly what they're doing, going to the North to tell people there what a beautiful country Ireland is going to be and you'd be mad not to be Irish.

On the train, my father is looking out the window with his tweed cap still on. It looks like the journey doesn't take very long, because they're already getting off the train again, walking along a country road crossing the border with cows in the fields and people following them. They walk right into the North and nobody can stop them. They get to Newry where they make some speeches with a small crowd of people listening to them and two officers from the Royal Ulster Constabulary watching with their hands behind their backs.

Then they arrive in Belfast. My father and the other men and women with him take placards and banners from the boot of a car and erect them on a street of red-bricked houses. Gearóid, the leader, speaks through a megaphone at a group of bystanders, mostly children and dogs who have nothing better to do than to watch people coming to make noise. The bystanders look like they're not really that interested and there's no need for the megaphone. My father is walking around with his limp, trying to sell copies of the Aiseirí newspaper under his arm and handing out leaflets to anyone who is willing to take one. Leaflets with drawings of bomber planes throwing down green fliers with the words 'Speak Irish' written on them. It was the Germans bombing the British cities and the British bombing the German cities and the Irish bombing everywhere with leaflets for the Irish language.

It was their crusade to Belfast. My father has told me many times before, that it doesn't matter if they don't listen, because sooner or later they will see the truth and join in. They'll all be with us one of these days. They told the people of Belfast that your language was your homeland. That's why the Loyalists in the North were so lost and confused, because they had no homeland of their own, only keeping with Britain across the water. They were afraid to be Irish, but once they realized that Ireland was a country with its own language, just like France or Germany or Israel, then they would be delighted with the idea. They would soon be rushing to join us and the whole country would be united again. All the Loyalists would be speaking Irish. Nothing was more certain. It was all about persuasion rather than force. Even though it was funny to invite people into the republic of Ireland who hated the place, things would change soon when they saw how happy we were in the south. One of these days the Loyalists would no longer be afraid of admitting that they were Irish underneath.

But then the RUC policemen had enough of Gearóid and his followers on the streets of Belfast, making speeches about the Queen of England and passing around leaflets of Irish bomber planes and giving out free stamps of the red hand of Ulster crossed out with a big black X. So they arrested Gearóid, the leader, and put him in Crumlin Road jail for a while to think things over. When he was released and expelled at the border, long after my father and the others had gone home, they told him never to come back, even though he was born in Belfast and grew up there.

After that, Gearóid was so angry at being kicked out of his own country, that he vowed that the next time he would go back, it would be with a hundred thousand armed men behind him. He went around telling people that they were still a cultural organization, but very soon they would be mobilizing an army.

When the Second World War started and my mother was still trapped in Germany, the papers were saying that the Germans would invade Britain and Ireland as well. De Valera, who was the Taoiseach at the time, kept Ireland neutral and made sure that the Irish people would not be dragged into the war on the side of the British or the Germans, for the Allies or the Nazis. The Irish had just liberated themselves from the British and they didn't want to get into another war. It was somebody else's fight, and we should keep out of it.

There were some people like Gearóid who wanted the Germans to invade Ireland. He was going around the country, telling soldiers in the Irish army that when the Germans arrived, they should not resist but join in with them. Of course, they didn't want to be invaded again so soon after getting rid of the British, but if the Nazis were to come to Ireland, they would actually do us a lot of favours. According to Gearóid and his followers in Aiseirí, the Nazis would unite Ireland. They would sort out the problem of Northern Ireland and put an end to British imperialism for good. It would be replaced by Nazi imperialism, but we would have a United Ireland and it would be the Irish language and the German language which would dominate all around the country.

It was clear that they might have to hand over the Jews that were living in Ireland at the time. Some of the members of the movement were making speeches against the Jews. As long as the Northern question was sorted out and there would be no more bigotry and apartheid rule by Protestant Loyalists, they didn't care what happened to the Jews. It seemed like a simple solution, a moral compromise.

Back then, my father learned German and maybe that's why Gearóid liked him and gave him a job as treasurer of the party, as his right-hand man. My father loved German culture and dreamed of Ireland being a strong and vibrant nation once again. Like others in the party, they believed that Ireland needed a strong leader who would set aside all the self-doubt that riddled the country and still made it half-British. When it became clear that Hitler already had too much to deal with elsewhere and that Ireland was the last thing he needed to add to his problems, Gearóid and others in the party began to despair and think the Northern Ireland question would never be solved. The golden moment was gone. Because they had to do it alone without any help from outside, Gearóid then went around saying to people in private that he was going to move towards an armed revolution. He canvassed for new members, saying officially that it was exclusively a cultural movement, but quietly he was telling them the opposite, that he would be arming the movement very soon, while Britain was still at war and the last thing Churchill would need is another sideshow with the Irish.

Gearóid wanted to show that his party was the one to be feared most in the future. His party was responsible for damaging the Gough monument in Phoenix Park and also for a riot outside the Metropole cinema on O'Connell

Street in which there was a baton charge by the Gardai. The Aiseirí newspaper talked about war preparations in Ireland and Gearóid was making speeches about going back up to Belfast very soon with force of numbers, armed to the teeth. But the first weapons they actually got in their fight to liberate Northern Ireland were not rifles but hobnail boots. Hobnail boots and rebel songs. It was said that young members of Aiseirí had begun to act like the Brown Shirts, going around disrupting other peaceful party gatherings by kicking onlookers in the shins and ankles. There was quite a bit of kicking going on at the time and it was said that De Valera's party, Fianna Fáil, had introduced the hobnail boot into Irish politics. They had their own gangs going around the country making an awful racket as they went through the streets. Some people said it was all just schoolboy stuff and that Ireland was never likely to imitate Germany. They said that Aiseirí was insignificant, but maybe they were missing the point because Ireland was lucky that Aiseirí never came to power, that Gearóid never got his hundred thousand pairs of hobnail boots together, unlike the Nazi party in Germany.

My father says it's unfair to accuse the Irish of things that never happened. But when it was clear that the Nazis were not coming to Ireland to solve the Northern problem, Gearóid began to talk about mobilizing. In desperation, he began moving the party towards the physical force ideology. And at that moment, there was a crisis in the movement. My father and some of the other senior members of the party organized a putsch. Gearóid's leadership was brought into question, because they didn't want to go along with an armed struggle. They still believed in a peaceful, non-violent, cultural movement, based on persuasion and openness. They became uneasy when they heard the reports of hobnail wars.

It was mostly the people from Cork who initiated this putsch, calling for a meeting in which they would announce that they had lost confidence in Gearóid as a leader. Was it a party of physical force or cultural persuasion, they demanded to know. They could not be both. It was either hobnail boots or poetry, violence or creativity. The Cork faction knew how creative violence and resentment could be, but they didn't want it.

When Gearóid got news of the impending putsch, he didn't wait for them to call a general meeting and expelled all the doubters from the party before they got a chance to speak. He went around to all the people who had planned the putsch and individually accused them of betrayal. He struck them off the register and said they were non-members. They had gone soft, he announced in a speech to an assembly from which they were now barred. The betrayers had become like all the other Irish people, unable to see the vision, unable to obey. But that only made matters worse and eventually the entire Cork membership resigned from the party and stopped paying their contributions.

I know what it was like for my father to lose his best friend. Gearóid would not speak to him any more. It must have been like the time that Packer froze me out, a time of great emptiness. He must have felt like he was drowning, or suffocating, walking around Dublin with his briefcase like an invisible man and his best friend walking past him in the street.

After that, the Aiseirí movement fell apart. Things had moved on and De Valera was saying all the things about Northern Ireland that the Irish wanted to hear. There was no need for Aiseirí any more and people drifted away into other parties. My father still had lots of energy left for Ireland. He still wanted Ireland to have lots of new inventions. So one day he went to see Gearóid and asked him to be friends again. It was like the moment when I went into hospital to see Packer after his motorcycle accident and we put the silence behind us. My father could not bear to be outside in the cold any longer and when he was assured that Gearóid would put aside any physical force, he was happy to rejoin the party.

So that's how the party came to an end, with the two of them, Gearóid and my father, as the last remaining members. Gearóid still went on publishing his paper and my father wrote for him. They kept having meetings in empty, unheated rooms on Harcourt Street and my father took down the minutes, even though it was only the two of them left under the naked light bulb. They continued to make speeches, but they had become an insignificant movement.

My second name is Gearóid, which means that I was called after the leader of the Aiseirí Party. Maybe it was lucky for Ireland that they never came to power. But as the party fizzled out, my father and Gearóid both decided to take the struggle inside, into their homes. What they could not achieve politically, they would achieve inside the family instead, where they could create the perfect republic with strong leadership. Gearóid got married and had lots of children. When my mother came over to Ireland from Germany and met my father, he got married too, and started the German-Irish family. The language war went indoors. Gearóid and my father did their best to outdo each other. They taught their children how to make sacrifices for Ireland. My father started with his eldest son,

Franz, and broke his nose one day for bringing English into the home. Gearóid did the same with his eldest son, who once had an abscess in one of his teeth, but because the dentist could not speak Irish, he took him home again and left him in pain.

My mother began to change my father and he no longer believes a lot of the things he believed in then. Sometimes he speaks to me and says he made mistakes. He wants me to forgive him and not to make the same mistakes. He wants to make sure I don't go up to the North of Ireland and join the IRA, because that would mean that our family had learned nothing, either from Irish history or from German history. He wants me to remember that he was against physical force, and even though he lost his temper sometimes out of frustration and idealism, everything he did was for us and for his country. He embraces me and I feel suffocated by the feeling he has for me. He says I'm going to correct all his mistakes. Because that's what fathers are for, so that sons can start again and make different mistakes.

I find it hard to talk to him, and it's hard to be friends with him, but when he smiles and goes back down the stairs into the front room, I can only think about all the things he made for us, the wooden toys, the trips he made with us, down to Connemara and over to Germany. I think of all the walks we went on and the camera he once bought for me on my birthday. It wasn't a real camera, but I kept taking photographs when we went down to the seafront. I clicked my camera and the photographs stayed in my head, photographs of my mother smiling and pointing out at the washing line of yachts in the bay, of my father with his hand up to shield his eyes from the sun, of the sea and the dog that barks at the waves, of people walking along with ice cream cones. We came across the ice cream van parked by the side of the road with the name Mister Softie. My mother bought us all an ice cream cone with drop of red jam in it and I took a photograph of Mister Softie inside his van. The engine was running all the time to keep the refrigerator going, so we could smell the ice cream and the seaweed and the puff of diesel fumes, all at the same time. It was a hot day and everybody was wearing summer clothes and trying to keep themselves cool. We even saw a Garda patrol car parked nearby with the windows open and two uniformed Gardai inside with their hats off, eating ice cream cones as well. They smiled when I took a photograph of them. Then my mother and father were laughing at the sea again, and I will never lose those photographs because they were made with a toy camera.

Seventeen

There is still no news from Stefan. No postcards, no message, no sighting in public. Tante Käthe has arrived in our house with shadows around her eyes, as if she's been crying all the way over from Germany. She has come to see the country where her son has gone missing. My mother talks to her in the front room, trying to convince her that Ireland is not such a fierce place as you might think, that the mountains are soft and the people are soft and that Stefan is so overwhelmed by the landscape that he's just forgotten to write home. But Tante Käthe looks at the rocks, the waves, the wide blue bay and the mountains behind the city, and to her they are all things that prevent Stefan from coming back home.

I am an optimist like my mother, so I keep thinking of Stefan alive, walking through the fields in the West of Ireland, kicking a tuft of grass into the air and scoring a goal between two gorse bushes, following a cattle trail and stepping through the gaps in the stone walls. Stefan, the inward man, on the run from his father, inventing a new identity for himself so that he will be given refuge. I call him the Playboy of the Western World, because he's made up a story for himself, a story where he can go underground and disappear. I know he's come to the big Irish mirror, the sight of the Atlantic ocean, where everybody sees their own reflection.

Tante Käthe hardly eats any of the sandwiches or the cakes that my mother makes. She sits forward in her chair when the Gardai arrive, as if she will have to stand up at any minute and go with them. They speak slowly to her in English to make sure that she understands. They accept a photograph of Stefan that she has brought with her and they agree that it might be a good idea, in time, to place a few posters in the shops and petrol stations around the country, but it's hard to know where. They ask if Stefan was of an unhappy disposition. Was there anything that he might be running away from. They explain that they are still actively pursuing the disappearance, but there is little more they can do. It makes no sense to broadcast any further missing person messages on the radio and there is nothing to be gained from starting a full-scale search, because nobody would know where to look first. When the Gardai leave again, my mother and Tante Käthe both come out of the front room as if Stefan's disappearance has brought back all the other tragedies of Germany, all the hurt and longing which they have had to suppress all these years since they last met in Mainz.

To cheer everyone up, my mother talks about how safe Ireland is and how she was able to cycle around on her pilgrimage without ever being bothered or being afraid of anyone. Ireland was like a fairy tale when she arrived first. Tante Käthe remembers all the letters that my mother sent back, how you could leave your belongings on a rock while going for a swim and nobody would take them. It was a religious country, full of people who stopped to bless themselves as they passed by a church. My mother wants Tante Käthe to see the place for herself so that she will be less worried. They both take the bus into the city to have coffee in Bewleys, to look at the stained-glass windows and the three-tiered trays of cakes on each table. My mother comes back and imitates the way that the waitress in her apron says 'Did you have any cakes, Madam?' with a small pinched mouth. My father becomes a tour guide again and offers to drive them down to Glendalough to see the round tower and I think they want Tante Käthe to be glad that her son is missing in Ireland, not somewhere else.

'He doesn't understand the sea,' Tante Käthe says.

Everyone knows that Stefan is a strong swimmer, but that doesn't mean he can't be tricked into swimming somewhere that looks calm, but which has dangerous currents that can tow even the best athlete in the world out to sea. My mother always told us to find some local person and inform them we were intending to go for a swim, because you could never tell what the conditions were like around the west coast. I always thought it was funny to go up to somebody and say we were going for a swim, because they might look at me in a strange way and say: Good for you. And good luck to you. Now she tells Tante Käthe that she gave Stefan the same warning and that surely means he is careful and that everyone from Spanish Point all the way up to Bundoran knows about every time Stefan has gone for a swim.

'The Atlantic. It's not like a big swimming pool,' Tante Käthe says, and you can see her imagining things that have not happened yet. She has the same nightmare factory that my mother has, from the war and the bombing. They are both still in the pre-calamity moment, thinking of bombs in mid-air that have not fallen yet, of murders that have not happened, of pre-drowning stillness when the sun is going down and gives the sea a peaceful look that cannot be trusted. Even though my mother has been living in Ireland for a long time and has got used to the Irish truth, she still can't help thinking that no matter how many good things have happened in the meantime, something bad is on its way in the end.

My mother asks me to tell Tante Käthe about my trip to the Aran Islands and how safe it was there. She takes out the diary and shows off all the postcards that Franz and I sent home when we went on a cycling trip around Ireland alone. She wants us to tell the whole journey, how we cycled down to visit our relatives in West Cork one summer and stayed in youth hostels along the way, how we sent a postcard home every morning, just like my mother did, sending daily letters home to Kempen when she arrived in Ireland first. She points out the map and the route we followed in red pencil, with little green flags in all the places where we stopped. There are notes in the diary on all the distances we travelled, including the mileage we travelled one day when we took a wrong turn and had to come all the way back again. The distances were all added up and the total mileage was written at the bottom of the page, underlined and followed with exclamation marks to show how impressive our journey was.

We told Tante Käthe about the most beautiful sight of all, the Rock of Cashel, how you come cycling around the bend and the ruins of this monastery just come into view as if you're the first person to discover it. We told her how we had sent Stefan down that road to Tipperary to find it for himself. We described how we cycled against the wind along the road from Urlingford, how Franz was always ahead because he was a stronger cyclist and never lost his energy, how I was always behind because I had the weakness and wanted to lie down by the side of the road, until Franz came back to encourage me and the energy returned to my legs when we came around a bend and saw the stone monastery clustered on the top of the rock. I forgot my weakness and cycled urgently back in time, as if I remembered it, as if I had been here before, hundreds of years ago.

Tante Käthe listens to every detail, how we prepared for the journey, how my father discussed the route with us, just like he did with Stefan, pointing out all the towns on the map that were of interest to us. My father didn't say much about the town of Leap where he was born and brought up with his brother Ted, but he told us where our relatives were living in Tipperary Town and Middleton and Skibbereen. He sat down with us and told us how he cycled from Dublin to Leap to see his mother while he was a student and could not afford the train. I heard him talking about his own life for once, without looking into the future. I heard him telling us about the time he went swimming once near Glandore and his brother, Onkel Ted, had to rescue him when he got into difficulty. He told us how he remembered seeing British soldiers along the road. He remembered hearing about an officer in the Auxiliaries, the Black and Tans, who was thrown out of the pub in Glandore for being so drunk and abusive and came back with a hand grenade which he threw onto the roof of the pub, but it rolled back down again and exploded right beside him, and he was killed by his own rage. He remembered hearing gunfire in the hills behind Leap. He told us how he saw Michael Collins stopping to visit friends in Leap, right across the street from where they lived, on the afternoon before he drove on to Béal na Bláth where he was killed.

We sat in the front room on the evening before we started the journey and it was strange to think of my father as a boy in short trousers. My mother made sandwiches and cake that would last us about four days at least. It was long before I started earning my own money at the harbour and my father calculated the amount we would need per day, the amount he used when he cycled all the way down to West Cork as a student. Then he added a shilling on top to make sure we would not go short. Franz was in charge of the money and he wanted to spend as little as possible, to bring back as much as we could so that my father would be impressed and would allow us to go on another journey because we knew how to live on nothing.

The night before we left on that big journey, he told us a story that he wanted us to keep with us for the rest of our lives. It was the story of the landlord and his fiery carriage.

In the towns of Leap and Glandore and Union Hall and Skibbereen, all around that area of West Cork, there was a story going around for a long time about a landlord whose carriage was seen passing by, on fire. It was like an Irish nightmare that kept coming back whenever it was getting dark or when there was a storm coming and the trees were beginning to sway in the wind. Children were afraid of seeing it and the people around West Cork could not put the fiery carriage out of their minds because it went back a long way in Irish history and was passed down through generations. Stories were the only way of remembering things, and they would often tell this one of how they looked up suddenly to see the flaming carriage speeding across the side of a hill at dusk. Some said they caught a glimpse of the flames in the woods, crackling and throwing off sparks. The sound of hoofs would come past them along the road without warning, and they would look up to see the flaming carriage rushing away across the lonely landscape towards the coast. The horses would be seen charging into the sea to try and put an end to it, but nothing could extinguish the flames, just as nothing could extinguish a story that came from the truth. Each time it went away, it always came back again with the landlord trapped inside his burning carriage, sitting in the back, staring with his dark, guilty eyes out through the flames at the people he had treated with such cruelty.

My father says he saw the carriage once when he was very small and he will never forget the look of horror in the landlord's eyes, condemned for ever to burn in this travelling hell for his past injustice towards the people. My father never believed in legends. He never tried to scare us with ghost stories, only real facts. And there was something about this story that was based in fact, something more than just a bit of folklore from a time when people had no television, and these stories were the only way that facts could be transmitted and kept in your mind. He said it was a story like the Flying Dutchman, a story that some Irish composer would make into great, world-famous opera one day. I remember how, on the night before we cycled to West Cork, he opened the glass bookcase in the front room and said there was something he wanted to show us, something to do with this fiery carriage.

He took out a small, thin notebook with a black cover. It was very old and worn, with rounded corners and a few age spots. He wanted us to hold it in our hands, Franz first, then me. He pointed to the calendar at the back from the year 1892 and said it was a very valuable document, not like the book from Mainz that my mother has in the oak trunk, but valuable in a different way because it tells the story of Ireland, a story that should be kept safe and should never be taken out of the house because it might be lost. The writing inside belongs to my great-grandfather, Taidhg Ó Donabhain Daill, Ted O Donovan Blind, the land surveyor who was not blind himself but descendant of a blind man, and decided at one point to start collecting all the names of places in the Irish language so that they wouldn't disappear. My father showed us the lists of place names around West Cork where he grew up and says you could follow your way along the coastline by these names. Every inlet, every harbour, every cliff and every rock is written down in the old handwriting and we're lucky he wrote with a lead pencil because that doesn't fade like ink.

He's shown me this book a number of times since then. There are names like *Carraig Árd* and the English translation beside it, High Rock. *Carraig a'choiscéim*, the rock of steps. The rock of two women. The rock of seals. Dead man's rock. There's even a rock called *Carraig a'chaca*, the rock of shit, which looks like a white skull because of the seagulls and cormorants. Some of the places have notes in English on distances and dangers around the coast. Descriptions of how the land looks like an elbow or a foot or goat's udder, coves that look like a short thumb and forefinger going out into the sea. The distances between Sherkin Island and Cape Clear Island. My father reads out the words of his own grandfather: 'No landing places south sides – the cliffs are too high. Strong currents. I had to stay in Cape Clear one time 10 days.'

The book also had a lot of proverbs that were collected by Ted O Donovan Blind along the way and my father reads out the very last.

'*Trí fithid bean nucht a chuirim chugat, agus mo bheannacht féin chomh maith.* Three score naked women I send you, and my own blessing as well.'

He laughs and explains how the word in the Irish language for a naked woman sounds exactly the same as the word for blessing. He says you can explain this in German or in English, but there are some jokes that can only be laughed at in Irish.

My father lets us hold his ancient book, in the same way that my mother allows us to look through her ancient book. They want us to feel close to the time in the past when these books were printed or written. They want us to be witnesses. They want us to be time-travellers, living in the past, sometime in the nineteenth century in West Cork, or even further back in the seventeenth century in Mainz. They want us to keep all that history in our heads. But you can't remember something that you have not seen with your own eyes. You can remember people talking about things that happened long ago, but you can't remember things that you have not witnessed.

The last thing my father showed us from his little frail book was one particular name of a place along the coast, not far from where they lived. It's called Toehead. It came from the Irish name Ceann Tuaithe, which means headland. Along the coast road out of Skibbereen, he explained, not far from Glandore, we would be coming across this headland which we would never forget because of the extraordinary view. There was nothing much out there now, he said, only sheep grazing. But there was a time around the great Irish famine when three hundred families were living on that headland. My father reads out the small note after the name.

Ceann Tuaithe – Toehead. Around 300 families lived here. All evicted. Barren place now.

My father told us there were stories going around that some people were driven off the cliffs. After the great famine in Ireland, the British government introduced a new policy which was intended to put an end to unproductive farming. It was a bit like the collectivization in Russia under Stalin, my father said. There was a lot of trouble in Ireland when people decided to stop paying their rent and were evicted by landlords. The Congested Districts Board was set up to alleviate poverty and bad living conditions. But there was also a policy of assisted emigration and land clearances. My father talked about evictions and a law called the Gregory Clause. He said the people of Toehead were evicted and Ted O Donovan Blind wrote down the name in his notebook so that it would not be forgotten. The story he heard as a boy was that evictions were carried out by gangs under police supervision. They would wreck the cottages to make sure they could not be re-inhabited. Some of the thatched cottages on the headland were set on fire. And that's how the story of the landlord and his fiery carriage emerged, when the flames from the roofs of the cottages were carried by the wind and as the landlord passed by on the road to see that the job was done properly, his carriage caught fire and he was condemned for ever by the people to live in his travelling hell.

I remember my father telling me this story. But you cannot remember things that happened before you were born. I can only remember what I have seen for myself. I remember that we cycled all the way from Dublin, stopping at hostels and staying with relatives in Tipperary and Fermoy, right down to Skibbereen. I can remember finding a packet of cigarettes that somebody had dropped on the ground. We ate the last piece of cake outside a shop near Fermoy. We saw a truck that had crashed outside a public house on the road into Clonakilty. I can remember that it took six days for us to cycle to Cork City and it was raining when we got there. There was nobody we knew living in Leap, but we got off the bikes to look at the house where my father grew up. It was covered with ivy. When I got on the bike again, my trousers were stuck to my legs and it was almost impossible to cycle. It rained so hard that we could not even see where we were going and had to blink all the time to keep our eyes clear. We stayed in Skibbereen with Tante Eileen for a few day, our clothes and our rucksacks hanging in the kitchen over the stove to dry. I can remember her house with a crooked floor. The front of the house had subsided because of years of flooding and the room was at an angle. I remember how it felt like being on a ship, tilted to one side. You could roll a penny down from one end to the other, towards the window.

It was only on the way back that we stopped at Toehead, but there was nothing much there. It's just a piece of grassy land going out into the sea. Hard to believe that 300 families once lived here. There must have been so many people walking along the roads in those days. It must have been busy as a city, and now it was all emptiness. There was nothing at all on Toehead, only a few houses at the foot of the slope going up. Barren place now, I remembered reading in the black notebook. There was nothing else for us to remember. We went right out to the tip of the headland and stood looking out over the cliffs going down on each side of the headland. We saw seagulls diving down into the water. We saw lines of foam on top of the waves. Boats were going out fishing from the harbour at Union Hall. A man with a pitchfork on his shoulder was walking inland with his dog, as if he was the last person left alive. There was a strong wind up there because it was so exposed to the Atlantic. When you shouted, the wind just whipped the sound of it away out to sea and made you speechless. The noise of wind in my ears made it impossible to hear anything. At one point I thought I heard people shouting and crying. I thought I heard the sound of hoofs and looked up to see if it was the landlord in his fiery carriage, but I knew it was an illusion.

I had the weakness, like an ache in my legs, and lay down on the grass in a place that was sheltered from the wind. Franz stayed looking out across the sea while I lay on my back looking straight up at the sky and the small white clouds going by very fast above us, as if the land was moving under me. I was floating on my back, head-first inland. I wondered how much you could remember and where the line is drawn between memory and imagination. Could you remember things that you have not seen, could you re-imagine things that you were told and relive them as if they happened only yesterday? I knew that I was lying on the land where people had been evicted long ago before I was born. I could imagine them alive. I could imagine the smell of turf smoke drifting on the wind and I could imagine the sound of people talking in Irish all around Toehead. I closed my eyes and listened to the wind and the sound of the Irish language all around me like a blanket.

I didn't want to go anywhere. I didn't want to get back on the bike again because I had cycled so much that I was tired and wanted to stay in one place for the rest of my life. I felt the weakness, like an ache in my legs. I was paralysed and wanted to be left there. I didn't care if it rained or got dark, I was ready to give myself up and surrender. I must have fallen asleep for a moment, because I heard my brother's voice calling me and saying we should move on before it got too late. I woke up and didn't even know where I was or what time it was or where I was in history. I opened my eyes and saw nothing but the sky and the clouds in front of me, moving at great speed away out into the sea.

'Come on,' Franz said. 'We want to get back to Middleton before dark.'

I got back on the bike with stiff legs. I was thankful that we were going downhill, off the headland for once. We stopped and turned around one last time to look at the view. It was unforgettable, with only the birds and the sheep and the Atlantic ocean spreading out like a big flat mirror.

On the night before Tante Käthe goes back home to Germany, Onkel Ted comes out to the house and my mother has baked another cake. Onkel Ted tells Tante Käthe that Stefan would soon be back, please God. We would all pray for him, and it would not be long before he would be in touch again. Onkel Ted was able to speak calmly and trust in the future. He's good at speaking German and even when Tante Käthe says she's afraid of what's happening in Northern Ireland and all the car bombs that are starting to go off, he listens to her and lets her talk out her worst nightmares. She's afraid of war and bombing coming back. She's afraid Stefan might have gone up there by mistake and that something has happened to him, like the German nightmare factory. She can't believe that the violence in the North will not spread all over the country and that Stefan will not be caught up in it.

But then Onkel Ted's calmness spreads all around the house and even the worst fears start floating away like music. Everyone becomes weightless when he speaks. He tells her that history is being repaired in Ireland, and that even though the troubles have broken out in Northern Ireland, it doesn't mean we are all at war again. He tells her the story about Tante Roseleen, when she was a small girl and there was an ambush around the creamery where she lived near Cork, in a place called Kilumney. It was the Black and Tans on one side and the IRA on the other. The family had fled from the house but when they came back, there were bullet holes in the walls. The bullet holes were never filled in or plastered over, so when Tante Roseleen was growing up and playing outside the creamery, she used to hide sweets in them.

'Sweets in the bullet holes,' Onkel Ted says.

It's what children do with the history of their country and all the bad things that have happened in the past. All over Europe, there must be children doing the same thing. Wherever there are bullet holes and bomb damage, there will also be children filling the holes up again, sticking their fingers in or putting in little stones, hiding their sweets and making up stories around them. I can see my mother and Tante Käthe both smiling with tears in their eyes, because the story of the bullet holes is so sad and happy at the same time, because children forget the real damage that was done and start repairing things with their imagination.

Eighteen

The harbour is quiet. For a moment it's like a silent movie and there's not even the sound of a distant engine to be heard. The world has stalled briefly and all that's left are the tiny, insignificant harbour sounds, like the water underneath the boats, the squeak of a tyre fender when it's pushed up against the harbour wall, the creak of a rope being stretched to the limit, the little rattle and shake that it makes and the misty shower of water wrung out by the strain. The harbour goes into a daydream and all your faculties go to sleep.

The sun is shining across the water and the reflection is so strong that you can hardly see without tears. Even closing your eyes is not enough and you have to turn away. The old people are down from the nursing home to spend the afternoon on the quay watching the boats. The nurses are with them, making sure their blankets are tucked in around them in their wheelchairs, making sure the brakes are on and they don't roll away into the harbour without anyone noticing them gone. There is an old woman asleep with a kind of baker's hat on her head and sunglasses gone sideways on her face. An old man in a wheelchair beside her who keeps his hand up as if he's waving at somebody out at sea. There is a tall man who has to link arms with a nurse because he's always trying to run away. The nurses told Packer once that he escaped from the retirement home one day and got the bus into town and it was nearly midnight before he was found sitting on the pavement in the city, drunk and singing. One night they caught him with his trousers on back to front, trying to break out through the window. The nurses bring flasks of tea and coffee, and distribute fairy cakes. They tell us how mean the nuns are with their tea bags and their allsorts biscuits. They tell us about the boy who was working in the kitchen and got a whole pan full of boiling chip oil over his face and hands, screaming as they carried him out into the ambulance. They tell us about the famous old people who are living there now and how they are forgotten by everyone, because time moves on and leaves all these people behind.

Maybe this is how I know I'm only at the start of my life, because I see these old people at the harbour so often. They have the time to look back and re-examine everything they went through and try to correct all the wrong turns they made. I'm just trying to move forward and not think back about anything at all. I'm escaping from the past and want to have no memory, while they want to keep their memory as long as they can, wishing they could start again with a clean slate, like me, doing all the things they missed because they couldn't recognize their own luck at the time. They say old people experience a second childhood, and maybe that's when you become innocent at last, when you see all your own mistakes.

I watch Packer and Dan Turley coming back from fishing. Packer ties the rope against the ladder, then climbs up with the lobster box while Dan scoops out the water from the bottom of the boat. Tyrone is there as well, getting ready to go out fishing. Dan and Tyrone ignoring one another as if they didn't even exist, pretending to be so busy that they are actually blind and cannot see.

There has been a development in the past few days that has turned the harbour into a courtroom again. The missing boat was recovered by the harbour boys, out on the far side of the island. It was undamaged, left to bob up and down with no heavy wind or big swells that might have lashed it against the rocks. Dan Turley is grateful for getting it back, but there were clues left behind that have strengthened all his suspicions. An empty bottle of whiskey was found in the boat, which, they said, pointed the finger straight at Tyrone. Also, who else would have known how to find a way off the island once the stolen boat was abandoned out there?

Tyrone has been found guilty in silence. Everyone is staring at him, executing him with their eyes, though there's no proof at all that he's done anything and nobody can come out and say it to him directly. It seems almost better that way, because we can judge him privately, among ourselves, without the confrontation. It gives Dan the upper hand, morally. He can point the finger as much as he likes and Tyrone cannot defend himself. Tyrone is forever bad, while Dan is forever good. A fair trial would ruin all that. And then I do something to bring every-thing out into the open. Because Tyrone is the enemy of Dan Turley, I pick up a dead crab from one of the boxes on the pier and throw it down into the harbour. I have no intention of hitting anyone with it and only generally throw it in the direction of Tyrone. But that has always been my problem. It's just like the trouble with the fireman at Halloween. My aim is so good that the crab bends on the breeze and flies like a big accusation through the silent air and drops right down into Tyrone's boat, landing at his feet. The dead crab stands for all the unspoken words flying around the harbour. I move away, back towards the shed to make sure nobody suspects me. I can hear Tyrone muttering, looking all around to see what bastard threw it. He wants to defend his good name. Then he looks across at Dan Turley who has noticed nothing and remains totally unaware of the flying crab.

Tyrone pushes himself off the moorings and sculls his way past some of the other boats without starting the engine yet. He lifts his oar up to push off the harbour wall, giving the boat enough momentum to cruise silently out towards the harbour mouth. As he comes to where Dan is bailing out the dirty fishy water, he brings the oar around through the air as if he wants to decapitate him. He's taking the law into his own hands and I see the oar swinging, but Dan crouches down to pick something up from the bottom of the boat and it misses him. Tyrone places the oar back into his boat and starts the engine. Nothing has happened and the world carries on as before. Tyrone bends down to throw out the rotten crab, while Dan climbs the ladder up onto the quay. They ignore each other and the whole thing is beginning to look like an optical illusion. I know I threw the crab and I saw Tyrone swinging the killer oar, but maybe my eyes were deceiving me, otherwise the old people and the nurses sitting around would have noticed it too. I could have just dreamed it all. I could have miscalculated the distances in the glare of the sun. From where I stand on the pier, it may have looked like Tyrone was trying to kill Dan, whereas in fact he might have been miles away, well out of reach. Suddenly I don't trust my eyes any more and wonder if I have started making my own nightmares now.

But then Packer comes up to the shed and places the

lobster box on the ground in front of me, looking at me with big open eyes.

'Did you see that?' he asks.

'What?'

'Did you not see Tyrone with the oar? Tried to kill Dan, I swear. He was only that much away, only inches away from killing him.'

Of course I had seen it, but I thought I had imagined it. I knew what was happening at the harbour and how things would come to a head one day soon, but maybe I could not believe it until I was told by Packer.

'You should have seen him swinging the oar. Jesus.'

I told him the sun was so bright that I could see nothing.

'There's something happening here,' Packer said. 'This is not over yet.'

At last, I could begin to believe what I had seen myself, what I had caused myself, only because Packer was now saying it. It was invented through his words. When Dan came up the ladder and walked back towards the shed, he seemed not to be too concerned about it.

'We saw that,' Packer said to him.

Dan didn't reply. He just turned around and watched Tyrone making his way out to sea, bouncing on the waves, standing up straight in the back of the boat with his hand on the engine. It was Tyrone's trademark and you could recognize his silhouette anywhere by the way he stood up in the boat unlike anyone else. Dan had a rule that you should never stand up in the boat, because that is the most common way of asking to be drowned. The slightest gust or wave from the ferry could jolt the boat and you're gone over. There was no point in being a hero at sea. And now he was watching Tyrone standing up in the boat like he was on skis with a cigarette in his mouth and a bottle of whiskey in his pocket.

'He could have killed you,' Packer said, but it was not clear at all whether Dan had really noticed how close he had come to being hit. Was he living in an optical illusion, trying not to see reality? Voluntary blindness. Maybe it was nothing more than the usual animosity and Packer was only exaggerating like he sometimes does, making it part of the big story that he is inventing around the harbour.

'Bastard,' I heard Dan say through his teeth. 'He'll hooken drown one of these days.'

At that moment, I realized how I had become part of the war myself. I was the person who had pushed things closer to the edge. All the sound came back to the harbour and the moment of illusion was gone. A half-dozen motorbikes arrived on the pier at once and everything turned back to normal. The nurses blew the exhaust fumes away from their patients. The girls hopped off the back of the bikes and straightened their clothes, their hair. Packer stored away the lobster in the box and Dan went inside into the shed to lie down and listen to the news. It seemed to be forgotten again, as if nobody had any memory of anything happening.

Every evening after dinner, we started saying the rosary in our house for the safe return of Stefan. It was some time now since his mother had come to visit and there was still no sign of him. One evening after the rosary, I sat alone in my bedroom when my mother came in and stood at the window. She was starting to practise freedom and opened the window to smoke a cigarette, half outside the window and half inside. If my father came into the room, she could throw the cigarette away towards the beehives and pretend nothing was going on and that the smoke was some garden fire that was still smouldering somewhere at the back of the houses. To put us off cigarettes, my father once lit one and then blew the smoke through a white handkerchief so we could see the brown nicotine stain left behind.

When my mother had finished her cigarette, she stayed at the window while it was starting to get dark. So then I asked her about Stefan's father. I had been thinking about what he had told me very briefly about his father in the war, and now I was sorry I didn't ask him any more questions, because he might not come back and I would never find out. At first, my mother didn't want to talk about it. But there is always time for the truth in our house, she says, so she told me what she knew and what she had heard from Käthe.

Stefan's father had been studying as a chemist during the Nazi years, but sometime after Hitler started the war with Russia, he was taken into the army and was ordered to go east. They drove all night and all day, because the German army had gone far to the east, as far as the Ukraine. She remembers Stefan's father saying how he could not believe that the land could be so flat for so long. He said the drivers of the tanks and the trucks were given special medication called Pervitin that would keep them awake and driving for days, but it then made them exhausted and aggressive. The same drugs that young people are now using for recreation. The Nazis had a factory for mind-altering drugs to keep the troops going. The soldiers were drinking a lot as well and often you could see them asleep in the back of the trucks, with spittle dripping down on their uniforms, not interested in where they were going or what the landscape looked like.

Stefan's father loved travelling and he was excited about going somewhere new and seeing the little villages in the Ukraine with wooden houses and cows tied up outside. Women with headscarves in the fields with their children working on the harvest.

Stefan's father didn't see much of the fighting, although he did pass through villages that had been bombed or set on fire. He saw people being evicted from their houses and driven up the road in clusters, carrying their belongings. But the first indication that they had come close to the front was when they stopped at a makeshift barracks and he could hear the very distant sound of artillery fire. He must have been afraid and excited, my mother says, because she remembers that sound as well. It's a sound where you keep wondering how far away it is and whether it's coming closer or whether it's going away. She says that sometimes you try and convince yourself that it's moving further away when it's actually coming towards you.

The soldiers were getting drunk every night on the alcohol they had found in the small houses. Other soldiers said the real party was going on just east of the camp, and Stefan's father believed what they said. He didn't realize that the word 'party' meant killing. My mother doesn't know exactly how this happened, but at one point, while Stefan's father was patrolling through the forest close to the camp, he came across the killing himself. There had been gunshots earlier that morning, but it had become very quiet. When he came to the edge of the forest, he could see German soldiers and SS men out in the open. He saw women undressing and had no idea what this meant. Women of all ages with their children and grandchildren. A group of soldiers got the order to fire and the women and children began to fall backwards into a pit behind them. It took Stefan's father a moment to realize what he was witnessing. He ran away, back into the forest, and could not understand what he had seen. He knew it was wrong, but he didn't know what to do about it.

My mother says Stefan's father got back to the camp and felt he would be arrested for what he had seen. He was afraid to speak to anyone about it. He felt that what he had witnessed was a crime and that he would be found guilty for speaking about it. He was afraid that he might be killed for knowing the facts. So he kept it to himself and even when others were hinting that there was something going on, he was terrified that if he uttered a word in public, he would pay for it.

'He had the weakness,' my mother says.

I wondered if Onkel Ulrich might have thought it was an illusion or something he had fabricated in his own mind. Of course he knew it was a scene of horror, because he heard the sound of children screaming as he ran back into the forest. He didn't know how his legs even carried him, because they were gone soft like jelly. He could still hear the sound of weeping years later, like a sound that would never die down, like some kind of tinnitus that came back every time he heard a baby crying. He was like the landlord in the fiery carriage, condemned to hearing the sound of weeping for eternity.

I know what it's like to have the weakness, to be powerless and have no way of doing anything to stop what's happening. Maybe Stefan's father is like me, waiting for somebody who would tell him what he had seen. People often don't understand what they have witnessed until it has been made clear to them.

It was not long afterwards that they were sent further

to the east and my mother says he must have lost any sense of self-protection. He was shot in the leg almost immediately and taken to the field hospital. His knee was completely shattered and he never walked without a stick again. I remember when we were small and went to Germany, we saw him always sitting sideways at the table. My mother says he was glad that he had been injured. He didn't care about his leg as long as the nightmare would go away and let him sleep. But the nightmare never left him. It kept coming back again and again, as if he was seeing it for the first time and he wanted to run away again each time but couldn't.

After he got back to Germany, he thought of reporting what he had seen, going to the newspapers, but everything was controlled by the Nazis. He told his own family, but they were afraid of what they were hearing and begged him never to say anything out loud in the open or they would all be sent to the concentration camps. So he kept it to himself.

It was only after the war, when he got married to Tante Käthe, that he could speak about it. It was all out in the open and he found out that things were even worse than he had imagined as he learnt about the concentration camps. Everybody was trying to rebuild their lives and all they talked about was repairing houses and finding food. He tried to work really hard to undo this nightmare that kept returning. He didn't think of writing it down in a diary or turning it into a letter to somebody who would take the images away. And it was not something he could talk to his wife about every night either.

It was only when Stefan was growing up that he finally found the right moment to speak out. He could have kept it like a secret to himself, my mother says, but he did the best thing of all, more courageous than anything he could have done during the war that might have been futile. Onkel Ulrich told his own son. He took the biggest step of all long after the war, in peacetime. He took the risk of losing the affection of his son, the risk that he would be killed by his own son, the risk that his only son would never speak to him again.

So that's how Stefan inherited the history of his father and the nightmare of the forest massacre in the Ukraine. That's why Stefan cannot get rid of it either. And now I bear the image in my head as well. I know that Stefan can do nothing to un-remember it either, because it's stuck in his mind as if he had seen it himself. My mother says, there is nothing you can do to put this nightmare out of your mind. 'We have to invent ways of un-killing people,' she says.

At first I don't understand what she means. But then she explains that we have to bring all those dead people back to life again. It's the Germans who killed them, but it's also the Germans who will bring them back by remembering them. As long as only one person in the world remembers, then they are still alive and not quite dead yet. As long as there is still a trace of those people, however small, left in your memory, that's all that matters. My mother says it's a new German invention, keeping those murdered people alive. We can't be afraid of the past. The past is not a weakness and we have to think of ways of keeping those murdered people from disappearing. It's the hardest thing to do, she says, but they are our people and it's going to be a great talent, something the Germans are going to be the best at, the un-killing of millions of people.

Nineteen

My father believes that too much freedom is bad for you, so he's imposed a new curfew and tells me to be back home by eleven. I argue with him and say that freedom is something absolute, like human rights, something you can never have enough of. He disagrees and says it's something precious, something you have to be a bit careful with. He has a duty to protect me from the perils of freedom, even though I don't want to be protected and only feel like escaping. He says I'm living in a fantasy if I think the world will ever be free of rules. I tell him that people are fed up being obedient and he says it's the opposite, people are more obedient now than they ever were before, and it's harder to break the rules of freedom than it ever was to break all the rules of totalitarianism and imperialism put together.

'The tyranny of freedom,' he calls it.

He's become the family prophet now, warning us about the good times coming. He tells me about his first taste of freedom after Irish independence when he became a schoolteacher and cycled through West Cork, how that freedom was linked with the idea of working and rebuilding your country. My mother says she still remembers the first day of freedom from the Nazis at the end of the war when she cycled home through the mountains. It's like a special smell in the air, she says, like when you lean your head down into a pram and inhale the scent of a newborn baby's head.

My mother tries to talk to my father, but he says he stands by the rules. If I'm not back in the house by eleven, I can stay out on the street and become homeless, because he will not allow me back in. As long as I live under his roof, I have to be subject to his law. So she comes and begs me to play the rules a little longer, just to keep the peace.

'I'm not going to live under a curfew,' I tell her.

'Please,' she says, when I'm going out the door. 'Do it for me.'

So that makes it worse, because it means that if I come in late, I won't be breaking his law as much as breaking her heart.

Most of the time at the harbour, there is nothing happening and we're only waiting for the day to end. Even in the summer, after the sun goes down, it stays bright for a long time and people hang around smoking and talking. The motorbikes come and go, bringing the harbour back to life one last time. You wait for the last boats to come in and when they are all tied up, we still wait until the harbour is deserted. In the nursing home, you can see the patients being put to bed and the lights going out. Lights going on and off again when one of the old people calls for something or can't get to sleep. Sometimes you can watch the same nurses making their way from room to room, until only the lights in the corridors are left on, nurses moving along each floor with the late-night medical trolley. Cars keep coming around the bend and shining their headlights across the boats, lighting up the whole harbour just for a moment before racing away up the road. The ferry from the main harbour goes out and you can see it getting smaller and smaller on its way over to England, like a lantern fading away on the water. Sometimes you feel you can even see the curvature of the Earth, because the ferry is high on the horizon and then slips down behind it. The last of the motorbikes is gone and you can still hear it going through the gears, all the way through the streets, until I can only imagine the hum of it.

Everybody is gone now. I am the last person left along with Dan Turley, and I still don't want to go home until he locks up and walks away up the pier to his house. All the signs have been taken down and stored inside. The fish boxes have been cleaned and put away. There is nothing left to do and Dan is about to close the door when we hear the sound of another boat coming in. It's hard to see who it is, but then against the light of the sky it's clear by the silhouette that this must be Tyrone, a man standing up at the back of the boat, gliding into the harbour and flicking the butt of his cigarette into the water.

I should leave now but I stay for a few minutes longer, as if I have some kind of premonition that something is about to happen. As Dan switches off the light inside the shed and gets ready to lock the door, Tyrone comes walking up from the quay carrying a fish box in front of him. I get on my bike, ready to cycle away, but then Dan begins to mutter and curse again. If I wasn't there, if there was no audience, he would say nothing and just close the door, forget that Tyrone even existed and just walk away home. But I'm the witness, the supporter who brings out the worst in him, and I can hear him goading Tyrone under his breath until he finally drops the fish box in his hands and steps right up towards the shed.

'What did you say?' Tyrone shouts.

The mackerel come back to life in the box and slap around furiously for a moment. Before I know it, the two men move up to each other, cursing and growling, face to face. Then they begin to go at each other with fists. Suddenly there are no more words and it's just straight violence now. It's a real fight. Two old men trying to kill each other on the pier and nobody around to stop it.

'Go on you fuckin' buffalo,' Tyrone shouts.

There's blood on his mouth. He must have got a punch, because his face has lit up with a red colour that almost looks black under the harbour lights. Now I know why blood is red, because it's the most alarming colour you can imagine, the colour that makes your heart race. Tyrone is trying to get back at Dan, trying to connect a decent punch, but they have locked on to each other in a wrestling match, huffing with the exertion. It's a breathing war as they shift around the pier, each trying to drag the other down.

I want to leave, but I'm paralysed by what I see. I can see Dan's white cap lying on the ground, so I pick it up. I place it on the trellis outside the shed, afraid of going any closer. It seems like a nightmare that has been coming for a long time, but I can't wake up or walk away. Dan Turley and Tyrone gripping at each other, pushing back and forth, just breathing and groaning as if they will never let go. I can see spittle on Dan's mouth, foam around his lips. I can see the whiteness of his head and the mark left behind by the rim of his cap.

Against the remaining light in the sky, I see them embracing each other in a vicious dance, as if they are suddenly doing a waltz, moving from one side of the pier to the other, all the way towards the edge until they nearly go over the side into the harbour, then all the way back towards the shed, swinging back so fast that it looks like Tyrone is forcing Dan to sit down on the trellis. They seem to be completely unaware of where they are. Nobody sees any of this happening and the nursing home seems a million miles away, with everyone fast asleep. Every now and again a car lights up the fight for an instant, as they sway back to the edge of the pier and stop at the crane, then all the way back until they crash right into the side of the shed. Twice more, Dan's broad back slams into the shed before they fall to the ground just inside the door.

I don't know what to do to stop this. I'm afraid to intervene. And then I wonder if they're only fighting because I'm watching, if I go away they might stop and come back to their senses. They pick themselves up like small boys off the ground and instantly lock on to each other again, waltzing around towards me so that I have to jump away and pull the bike out of their path at the last minute. My mouth is so dry that I can't even say a word. Then I get on my bike and start cycling away to get help.

And then the fight comes to an end. I stop to look back and maybe I was right, that I'm only keeping the fight alive by being present. They let go of each other and I watch them standing there, leaning forward a little, with their hands on their hips, just breathing heavily.

'Just you fucking wait,' I hear Tyrone say, before he picks up the fish box and disappears away up the pier.

Dan finds his cap and brushes it off before putting it back on his head. He stands for a moment, staring after Tyrone with black marble eyes, unable to say a word because he's breathing so heavily. His mouth is open and there is spittle hanging from his chin as if he's got no energy left to wipe it off. I wait to see what he's going to do, if he's going to get the hatchet, but he doesn't. He locks the door of the shed, fumbling with the keys for a long while, unable to do it any more, and I want to run back and help him. He doesn't see me and I know he doesn't want me to talk about this to anyone. Then I finally see him wiping the spittle off his chin with the sleeve of his jacket and I cycle away.

By the time I get home, it's already too late and I find the door of the house locked and bolted from inside. It could only be little more than five minutes past eleven, but the curfew has fallen and my father has closed the fortress against me. I rest my bike against the side of the wall and look up at the windows, but all the curtains are drawn. The lights are out, as if they're all in a rush to prove that they are asleep. I can't ring the bell, so I wait outside for a while until my mother realizes that I'm back and sneaks down the stairs to open the door very quietly. My father doesn't hear her locking the door again, though there is a loud click as the lock jumps back into place.

We stand in the hallway for a moment. My mother likes this secrecy, as if I'm doing all the things she wishes she had done herself. She holds my hand and looks into my eyes for a moment.

'Is there something wrong?' she asks.

Maybe she can sense what I've witnessed. But I tell her nothing and we creep up the stairs like two thieves. I know the creaks on the landing and how to avoid them. We wave at each other in silence and go to bed.

I lie awake for a while thinking of what I have seen. I imagine what's going to happen next at the harbour and how it will end. I watch the light from the street throwing the shadows onto the wall of my bedroom. I see the fight starting again and again, like an endless film, Dan picking up his cap and wiping the spittle from his chin, until I'm exhausted and fall asleep, But even in my sleep I hear more shouting, right in close to me. This time I am no longer just a bystander. I can see the rage in Dan Turley's eyes. I can see his bottom lip pushed forward and hear him breathing. I can see blood on his neck, on his hands. I can see drops of blood on the pier, leading away to where Tyrone has gone to find an oar or something better to fight with. A trail of blood that you sometimes see along the pier after somebody has carried up a box of freshly caught mackerel. A trail of blood that you sometimes see on the street and wonder if it was a fight or an injured dog. I see Tyrone moving quickly around the pier with a broken oar in his hands.

'Come on yah fuckin' buffaloes,' he's shouting.

And this time he's coming for me. Tyrone swinging his oar around, aiming straight at me, pinning me back against the shed. I want to wake up, but I can't get out of this nightmare any more and I feel the oar hitting the side of my face. I can hear the sound of the wood echoing inside my head and when I wake up at last, I find that my back is right up against the wall of the bedroom. The light is on in the room and I can hardly see anything, except my father, standing over me, punching his fist down.

'You let him in,' I hear him shouting. 'That's treachery.'

I am blinded by the light overhead. I can see him in his pyjamas, without his glasses on, my mother trying to pull him back by the elbow, trying to stop him hitting me again. I can hear him gasping with the effort. I have no defence and I feel the punches coming one after the other and my head knocking back against the wall behind me. I feel myself sinking down under the blows, as if the oar is striking me again and again and my back is sliding down the side of the shed. Tyrone standing over me with a look of insanity in his eyes and Dan Turley holding him back to stop him from finishing me off.

It is all the punishment in history being passed on blow by blow, all the revenge and all the resentment going back for centuries, here in my bedroom. Nobody can stop it. My father is breathing so hard he can't speak. It's the breathing war. He rolls up his sleeves to do it better. I can see he has already taken his watch off. I can smell his sweat. As my eyes finally get accustomed to the light, I can also see that the whole house is up and the room is full of people, the entire family around me, with their hands together as if they are all praying for this to end.

'Peace,' my brother Franz suddenly calls out.

Then everything stops. There is silence in the house, as if somebody from outside has spoken and our family has begun to see itself for the first time. I see them crowding around my father, trying to help him out of the room, as if something terrible has happened to him. They ignore me and keep looking after him. They are afraid for him and worried because he's so angry and upset by what he has done. They know he will feel terrible about it and want him to sit on the stairs, to calm down and take in a deep breath.

'I want him out,' he keeps saying. He sits on the stairs for a moment, with everyone around him, as if he was the person who was attacked. I'm left sitting up in bed feeling my face and then I realize that my eyes are wet and I can't stop myself crying. I feel so guilty. I feel so hurt, so angry that I want to kill him. I feel like running away and never coming back.

My father gets up suddenly and goes down the stairs

to the front room. He says he's going to call the Gardai because there is an intruder in the house. If only my father could see how ridiculous this has become, calling the police to evict his own son. He is determined to make the call, right in the middle of the night, while my mother begs him to leave it till the morning. She puts her finger on the button to cut off the dialling tone a number of times, but then he fights her off.

'Yes, an intruder,' I can hear him saying out loud.

I'm afraid I will soon be homeless. I get worried about having to live for the rest of my life as an outsider. But then I hear the phone hanging up again.

'Think about it,' I can hear my mother pleading with him. 'You don't want him to be like Stefan, disappearing and never coming back.'

So then I leave the house. Before anyone can stop me, I call my father's bluff. While they are all still in the front room trying to stop him from calling the Gardai to our house, they hear the front door slamming. My mother runs out and I hear her calling me back, but I keep running down the road with tears in my eyes, saying to myself that I will never come back again because the whole house is like a wardrobe and if I don't escape now, I never will.

I walk the streets on my own. I spend some time back at the harbour, but then I have to keep moving, like the mackerel, because now I'm homeless. I walk all the way up the hill where I can look down over the whole city, like an orange bowl in the distance. I sit on one of the benches thinking how I want to go back and kill my father. I think of him with spittle on his chin, staring at me, out of breath. But then I can't live with the hate in my head any more. I can't hold on to my anger and I can't help wanting to forgive him again. I want to be friends with him and feel sorry for him. It's my fault that he lost his temper, and I'm glad I didn't retaliate. I'm glad I didn't do something like Stefan that I could not repair.

I look across the flat orange bay and think about my future, how I will soon escape and be free. It makes me want to think of all the good things my father has done instead. I think of how he made me a pair of stilts for my birthday one year. He produced them at breakfast and I was amazed that he could have made them in secret without me knowing anything. I'm not a child any more and I watch what's going on in the house all the time. But still he made them without anyone knowing, except for my mother. It was like a conspiracy of kindness. They were painted in blue, with the foot steps painted in red. I keep thinking about my father constantly trying to do his best, tricking us with great surprises.

On the morning of my birthday, before he went to work, he helped me to get up on the stilts in the hall. I had to lean with my back against the wall to get myself up onto them, and then I was suddenly looking down at my father smiling below me, telling me to give it a go, even though I was nervous of falling off. He was clearing the way so that I could walk through the hall, taller than anyone else in the house.

Next day, the war in our house came to an end. I apologized to my father, because I hated to see his hurt mind and my own hurt mind. I didn't ever want to see him breathing hard again. He was outside with the bees buzzing around him and when he came in and took the cage off his head, I told him it was my fault and I would be on his side from now on. I was going to keep his rules. It was peace at any price now. My mother negotiated another amnesty and the house returned to normal. We were all friends again and I had a pact with my mother, to keep my father happy, to escape in more creative ways that would not hurt him.

Some days after that, Stefan returned without warning. Out of the blue, he appeared as if he had never even been away and no time had gone by. I came back from the harbour and heard his voice in the house, like the voice of a ghost who had returned from the dead. I walked into the breakfast room and Stefan was sitting there, with my mother and my brothers and sisters all looking at him as if they couldn't trust their eyes. The brother we lost, the un-dead brother returned home.

At first there was more trouble because he had made everybody worry so much and my mother kept asking him how he could have been so thoughtless not to have sent at least some word home that he was alright. Stefan was annoyed when he heard that his name had been read out on the news and that he was classified as a missing person. Of course he went missing, but there was no need to go to the police, because he was only touring around for the summer and he didn't want to think about home. When my father got back from work, I could see that he was furious and it looked like he preferred Stefan to be still missing.

'How dare you come back like this?' my father said. He was speaking to Stefan the way he speaks to me. It looked as if my father was going to hit him like he attacked me in the middle of the night.

'We thought you were dead,' my mother said. 'Stefan, your mother was here, crying.'

Stefan went silent. It looked like he, too, was sorry he came back and felt like getting up and leaving again, maybe getting lost for ever this time. My father was waiting for him to apologize for causing so much trouble, as if that was all people ever had to do for the rest of eternity, to keep on apologizing to each other.

'I was trying to find myself,' Stefan said.

Maria could not stop herself from giggling, a spontaneous burst that came out through her nose, but my father said there was nothing to laugh about. He stared at Stefan and said it was a fresh answer. It was an insult to come back to our house and speak in such an impertinent way. The funny thing was that I think Stefan actually meant what he was saying, that he really was trying to find himself, because he had lost contact with the real world.

'We have imagined him back to life again,' my mother said.

She went over to Stefan and put her arm around him. She said our prayers were answered and we were so happy that nothing happened to him. It was a cause for celebration. First of all, Stefan would have to make a telephone call home to his mother and tell her that everything was alright. Then Stefan was going to have to eat something decent because he looked so thin. We would have to feed him properly before he went back home to Germany. My father forgot his anger and at dinner, Stefan told us about all the places he had been to, down in County Clare, listening to music and fishing with some of the men in the villages. From there he travelled through Mayo, through bogs that were like purple rugs, places where you thought you were the last man alive on Earth. In Sligo, he met young people from Belfast who brought him up North and we were all amazed that he was not afraid to go up there with all that was happening, the car bombs and the riots and the shootings. He said he sat in small pubs with people who were singing songs and learned some rebel songs himself. He said they played guitars like they were machine guns. A hippy song called 'Massachusetts' had been turned into an anthem of freedom fighting. They even took him to a riot and he threw stones at British armoured cars passing through the streets. He said he would never forget the sound of a stone against the green steel of a military Land-Rover.

Stefan got up and went out to find something in his rucksack. When he came back to the table he had a black object in his hand, which he then passed along to my mother.

'I was nearly hit by that,' he said.

'What is it?' my mother asked.

'It's a rubber bullet.'

My mother examined it. She had never seen anything like it before and held it as if Stefan had truly come back from the dead.

'You could have been killed,' she said.

She felt the weight of it in her hand. Everybody crowded around her to see for themselves. A souvenir of war. The souvenir from the world of rules and repression. I saw that it had a dent in the material and Stefan explained how it had hit the wall of a red-bricked house right behind him. He had heard the sound of it swishing through the air. We understood how lethal these plastic bullets could be because a boy had been killed only recently on the streets of Belfast by one of them. We passed the rubber bullet around and my father examined it thoroughly without saying a word.

'It's an improvement,' my mother said, but then she suddenly laughed and nobody could understand what she meant by that. 'It's an improvement on real bullets.'

Stefan said that was a good way of looking at things, from the opposite direction, from underneath.

'If it kills less people, then I suppose it must be an improvement,' he said.

And then we were all laughing around the table, and even my father joined in and said rubber bullets were a great invention because they saved lives. He handed it back to Stefan so he could put it away in his rucksack. My mother told him not to show it to his own mother because it would upset her very much to see it. She asked Stefan what his plans were, whether he was going to go back home now. Stefan said he had been to the Aran Islands. He had sat on the cliffs overlooking the Atlantic. You could go no further, he told us, and now it was time to turn back.

'You're not a missing person any more,' my mother said. She embraced him again as if he was her own son.

Stefan stayed with us for a few days more before going back to Germany. I went swimming with him, back to the secret place behind the terrace of white houses. I told him about the fight at the harbour. I told him about the fight with my father as well, and then he started telling me that before he left, he had hit his father and knocked him to the ground in the garden. He could still see him lying there, unable to get up with his injured knee. He told me that he walked away without helping his mother to pick him up, but now he felt sorry about that and wanted to go home and put all that right again because that injustice which he had done to his own father had begun to haunt him as much as the story which had been passed on to him from the war. He was going back because he and his father were part of the same history. It had not been possible to separate himself from that. He had lived in fear of making the same mistakes and now he wanted to be able to trust himself, to be free to make his own mistakes.

When he was leaving, my mother packed his bag with packages of barm brack for the journey. She was so excited about him going home alive, like a son returning after the war, that she had tears in her eyes, even while she was smiling. At the last minute, when Stefan was already standing at the door, she took out the ancient book from the time of Gutenberg and showed it to him. She had it ready for him wrapped in a thin blue see-through paper. She could hardly speak and without thinking about it, she put it into Stefan's hand. He had to take his rucksack off again to stow it away safely, wrapped up in that see-through paper, then placed inside a brown envelope and finally wrapped in a jumper to make sure it would not be damaged. She wanted him to take it home. She was determined that it should go back to Mainz now. It was one of the few things that survived the war and she wanted him to carry this ancient book with him because maybe Germany is where it was needed most from now on. She wanted to repeat all the help she had given people during the bad years. She wanted to make sure that it was all done without any payment. She wanted to return the book, not because she thought it didn't rightly belong to her, but because she refused to benefit in any way from a time of killing and hunger. She told Stefan to be very careful not to lose it, because it was very precious and would remind him that time goes back a long way.

Twenty

Now it's goodbye to the harbour and goodbye to the hurt mind. Packer and I are moving on. We've stopped hanging around, sitting on the trellis outside Dan Turley's shed. We've stopped going out in boats and we've stopped coming home with mackerel scales on our hands. We still go down there from time to time as visitors, but we don't work for Dan Turley any more and we don't get paid. There was nothing said, nothing official, no formal notice, just Packer and me deciding one day that it was the end of something, the moment of departure when you move out of the present and never turn back.

It was the drowning that changed everything. After Tyrone was drowned, we began to talk about the harbour as if it was in the past, as if we were no longer part of it. When the news went around about Tyrone's boat being found adrift one morning with nobody inside, it seemed inevitable to us, something we had quietly predicted long ago. It was the signal for us to leave. We could not help connecting it to what was happening in Ireland at the time. We heard the news on the radio every day getting worse and it sometimes looked like they were inventing new ideas for killing, new violence that had never been thought of before. It was bad justice all around. Internment without trial. Torture in police stations. People talking about the occupation and trying to balance up the justice gap with more injustice on all sides. Soldiers killed in roadside bombs. UDR men assassinated on their farms as they went out to milk the cows. A mother of six children murdered for helping a wounded soldier. It was the big hurt factory, and we went numb every time we listened to the radio or watched TV. It was hard to think of anything as 'now' or 'here' and we sometimes thought Northern Ireland was as far away as Vietnam, and maybe we only wished it was. We could never even find much to say about it and kept on doing our own thing as much as possible. But then we realized it was here all along at the harbour in front of our own eyes.

I could not get the drowning out of my head. It was the closest I had ever come to death and I remembered how I had once tried to drown a dog when I was still trying to learn how to hate. This was our own hurt industry. We had seen Tyrone so often, standing in his boat as he rode the waves, bouncing out across the water in the late evening like the silhouette of a skier, leaning forward a little with a cigarette in his mouth. Now we watched people going out searching for him along with the rescue services, a fleet of small boats checking all the inlets and beaches along the coast. We went out with them, although we were not sure if we had the right to be so concerned about him now, when we didn't care very much before. We joined the search from a distance. Boats from all the other harbours moving slowly across every inch of water, right along the bay into the city. There were crowds gathered on the pier, co-ordinating the search. People with flashlights late in the evening. People dressed in new oilskins and life jackets. People who only barely knew Tyrone standing on the rocks with binoculars. Everyone grouping together because they say we're all equals when it comes to the sea, we're all equals in front of death.

People continued coming down to buy fish. Sometimes a boat would come rushing back into the harbour, a man getting into a car, driving away at speed as if he knew something. Even the old people in the nursing home must have heard the news, because they were all at the windows, staring down at the boats coming and going all day, even when it rained, even after dark. All through the night, the beam of the lighthouse came around every half a minute or so, lighting up the field of silver water, and if you watched for long enough it would coincide with another lighthouse further away, shining across the bay at the very same moment.

There was no sign of Tyrone and everyone began to assume the worst. When his body was eventually found, given back by the sea one evening on the incoming tide, after dark when the water was turning pink, it only confirmed what everyone already knew. It was the blue light of the ambulance around the harbour that shocked us most, the blue light flashing across the boats, across the white faces of the men standing around like ghosts on the pier, across the dead windows of the nursing home. It was a tragic drowning that shocked the community all the more because people said they had seen it coming. They said he was an experienced fisherman who was well known and well liked in the area, one of the most familiar characters whose death would bring us all closer together.

We saw the funeral cortège carrying him past the harbour one last time on the way to the cemetery. There were two of Tyrone's oars slipped in alongside the coffin for him to be buried with. His coffin was like a boat which had been draped with ropes and fenders along the side. For the first time, we could see the full sadness of it coming right past us, with his family and his relatives and friends behind the hearse. We saw them crying, supporting each other as if they were going to collapse with grief. A woman with her hand over her mouth with her eyes red, full of tears. We understood for the first time that Tyrone must have had a life full of stories, objects that belonged to him, things that would be remembered by his people going right back to his childhood. They would keep him alive in their thoughts now and never let him go. We kept seeing funerals on TV, very similar to this one. Every time there was a death in Northern Ireland, we saw men carrying the coffin, bereaved women and children huddled together around the open grave. Sometimes the coffins were draped in flags, but mostly it was just the bare polished wood, carried along through the streets with a silent crowd in black following behind. We saw photographs in the newspapers of the agony on people's faces as if they could still see the dead person right in front of them and could not get used to the idea of them never coming back any more, only their clothes and all the things they owned left behind as if they had promised to be back soon.

Now, one of those coffins was coming right by the harbour and we were standing outside the shed, watching it going slowly by and stopping for a full minute, because they wanted to remember Tyrone going out in his boat one last time. We stood watching them moving on again and I turned around to see Dan Turley with his thin lips and his narrow eyes staring at the coffin and the mourners without a word. He was standing in the doorway of the shed, with the same hard expression in his eyes all the time, and I was wondering what he was thinking, whether he thought it could so easily have been his own funeral instead, if in death they were finally going to shake hands and put everything behind them. I wondered if he was just like us, all a bit like ghosts, like the un-dead left behind now on the pier while the hearse moved on up the hill around the bend by the nursing home, never to come back.

It was strange to think of the world returning to normal and the sound of motorbikes and buses passing along the main road on the far side of the nursing home, how the funeral cortège would still be holding things up here and there on its way to the cemetery. Dan Turley remained silent. He retreated back inside his shed. Packer and I stood looking out at the harbour and we knew the moment had come when we could no longer belong to this place.

'Goodbye to the hurt mind,' Packer said to me after a long silence. He said it like the line of a song. It was to become his new phrase, the one that would lead us away from all these things that were happening around us, not only here at the harbour but all over Ireland and elsewhere in the world. I could see that he liked saying it again and again, as if these were the only words left in our heads with any weight in them. So now it's goodbye to the mackerel and goodbye to the fish scales. It's goodbye to the wet ropes, goodbye to the smell of tar on the roof of the shed. Goodbye to the smell of seaweed and petrol and oilskins together in one mixture. Goodbye to the sunshine on the pier and goodbye to the special smell of red-lead, anti-fungus paint on the bottom of the upturned boats.

It's goodbye to the cigarette butts floating in the harbour and goodbye to the little coloured oil slicks that are left behind by the engines. It's goodbye to the sound of oars and goodbye to the squeak of fenders against the harbour wall and goodbye to the seagulls floating on the water.

Packer is always meeting new people wherever he goes and he's made friends with somebody who is a genius on the guitar and can sing 'Talking third world war blues'. He has begun to gather people around him who love music and has the idea of starting a band, even though none of us can play anything. They've been trying to teach me how to play the guitar, but I have no rhythm and don't trust myself to be listened to. I believe that if you sing or play an instrument, you become like a piece of glass and people can look right into your head and see everything, all your thoughts and all your memories, everything you've been trying to keep hidden all along. Once you open your mouth, you let everybody into your house to look around. I need to learn how to breathe first and then I'll be able to sing. I still breathe as if the air doesn't belong to me, and maybe it's always like that for outsiders, that you only borrow the air around you instead of owning it like everyone else. So they're going to teach me how to sing and breathe as if the air is my own.

At home, my father doesn't enforce the curfew any more. He doesn't ask what I do and what time I come home, because he is preoccupied with other things, with his bees, with translating books and writing more articles for the papers. He's been planning a business trip to Germany for the ESB, to buy a new shipment of high-voltage cables. He's been translating technical manuals for them and right now he's been given a big problem to solve for Ireland that does not involve any fighting or dying. It's a problem that none of the leading experts in the ESB have been able to crack, because it's about Britain and Germany.

The ESB generating station at Ard na Crusha was built by the Germans just after Irish independence, by a company called Siemens. It was well known that the Germans were the best at engineering, so they were brought in by the new Irish Free State government so they would build a generating station at the Shannon that would light up the whole country. As they were building a power station on the Shannon estuary at Ard na Crusha, the Germans began to have trouble getting the Irish workers on the scheme to work, and the German foreman once got a gun and went down to the barracks where the men slept and woke them up early with the gun pointing at their heads, saying that if they didn't come to work on time in future he would shoot every one of them with his pistol. He was so furious and had such a serious look in his eyes that they believed him and didn't think it was just a German playing a joke. So the generating station was finally built, even though everyone was saying it was a white elephant and the farmers all over the country didn't want ESB poles on their land. But now there was a new problem. The station had been in operation for years, and to complete the rural electrification scheme, it had to expand. In addition to the German transformer, the ESB bought a British-built transformer which was a little easier to bring into Ireland. There was no reason why a new British-built machine would not work with the German one. But when it was finally delivered and installed, the engineers at Ard na Crusha could not get them to work together. The two big machines were designed to work in series, next to one another, my father says, so that there would be a huge saving in power which would double the capacity provided for the national grid. It had taken months for the new machine to be imported and built up, but when the machines were asked to work together, they refused.

Senior engineers were sent down from head office in Dublin to carry out tests. They studied the manuals and went back to the beginning each time, to see if they had missed any vital steps. They could not understand how a machine could be so stubborn and they began to think it was something psychological, something to do with the war that made even the machines reluctant to make it up and put the past behind them, some basic incompatibility between the German and the British models. The Irish understood that very well, my father says, how a machine would resent the newcomer. Of course the engineers didn't put that down in the reports, but they did finally pass the problem back to head office saying they were baffled and could only conclude that it was a non-technical malfunction.

Experts were sent to Britain and to Germany to consult the manufacturers, but they came back no wiser. The British machine which had been bought at great expense was lying idle and only the German model was being used for the moment. It remained a mystery. All the leading engineers scratched their heads and passed the problem on, blaming the person who had made the decision to try and match two different makes like this in the first place. It was at this point that somebody remembered that my father spoke German and that there might be no harm in him having a go at it.

So he's been sitting at home every night, going over all the different reports, studying the tests that were carried out in Ard na Crusha as well as all the reports from abroad. Night after night, poring over the same documents and manuals, measuring and calculating everything mathematically. He doesn't believe that a problem can't be solved and doesn't believe that machines have a mind of their own or that nationality plays a part in electrical science.

'It's the ghost in the machine,' my mother says at the dinner table, and they both start laughing. My father says it's only Irish people who still believe in the supernatural and they will never solve anything if they remain in this pre-technical state. He says they still look at every problem from an emotional point of view, as if everything is personal. They have deluded themselves into believing that machines are possessed with nationalist features which make them unreasonable and uncooperative.

'The machine is a servant,' he says. He speaks as if he has discovered something about himself and us at the same time, as if it's suddenly become clear to him that he turned us, his own children, into machines when we were small.

'Under the right conditions, with no obstacles in the way, a machine will do as it is told in any language. This idea that a machine is like a donkey or a human with temperament is nonsense.'

Then for the first time in our lives around the table, we realize that he is speaking to us in English. The most basic rule to keep everything British outside the front door has been broken by himself.

'The Irish must step into the technical age or they will not survive,' he says, and we are shocked to hear these words coming from him in English. It should be a moment of freedom, but we feel rigid, almost wishing that he would keep to the rules no matter how absurd they have become. Franz is worried that my father might ask him a technical question and he won't know what language to answer in. We're still afraid to speak, so we would rather be silent and listen.

We are astonished at how natural he is in this forbidden language. He's a different man, more relaxed, more like other men in Ireland. Even though we are still afraid to join in, we admire the way he speaks with a soft Cork accent. For the first time in my life, I hear him speaking to us in his own language, putting everything in his own words, breathing in English. Up to now he's always been speaking to us in a foreign language, either in German or in Irish, languages that were never his own. Now he's speaking to us in his native tongue, the language of his childhood, the language of his memory, the language of his own mother. It's the language he went to sleep in when he was a boy, the language of stories and songs that he heard when he was growing up. Now I can understand what he really means to say, as if he's got his voice back after years of exile.

Night after night, he sits in the front room now, surrounded by sheets of paper and manuals all around him on the sofa and on the floor, speaking to himself in English and speaking in German when my mother goes in to try and help him, even though she has no idea what all these technical terms mean. She asks the most simple questions and makes him think about the problem like a child looking up at a plane crossing the sky. He walks around the house with the drawings in one hand and a cup of tea in the other. When he's outside on the roof of the breakfast room tending to the bees, he suddenly drops everything and runs inside to look at the manuals once more, with his bee-keeping gear still on. He's going around like an astronaut in another orbit. He doesn't see what's going on and he's stopped being on sentry duty, watching us all the time to see if we're breaking the laws.

He doesn't even notice that my mother has begun to start smoking. She has been giving German lessons to some of the students around the neighbourhood and one day, while she was teaching and smoking a cigarette at the same time, he came home and walked straight into the front room. My mother didn't know what to do with the cigarette in her hand and decided to give it to the student, who was only thirteen years of age, but my father noticed nothing, as long as my mother was not smoking. He was in his own world, just wondering why the ghost in the British machine still refused to talk to the ghost in the German machine.

And then one night he's cracked it. Long after everyone has already gone to bed, he wakes up the whole house, walking up and down the hallway in his pyjamas, slapping his hands together, with us on the stairs thinking he's gone out of his mind.

'It's fifteen past midnight,' he says, and he's smiling.

'It's much later than that,' my mother says.

'No, I mean clockwise and anti-clockwise,' he says. He's so happy that he wants to run out onto the street in his bare feet, but my mother closes the door and pulls him back into the front room, with all the lights in the house on as if electricity doesn't cost anything and Ireland is going to have too much of it. My mother says you can't run out naked like the man who invented the displacement of water in the bath. My father is buzzing with excitement because he's cracked the mystery that will bring peace between the machines. He can't stop walking up and down the room and back into the hallway, smacking his fist into his hand and then throwing the drawings up in the air as if they no longer matter. He's laughing at them all now. He tells my mother to get out the cognac and the special German biscuits, because he wants to celebrate and put on music.

'I was blind,' he says. 'I don't know how I didn't see it.'

He says the solution was so simple that everybody in Ireland missed it. It was so straightforward it was staring us all in the eye. He explains how both machines had a dial. Both the German model and the British model needed to run together at the setting of fifteen from midnight, but they could not see that the Germans had the convention of going clockwise and the British had the convention of going anti-clockwise, after midnight and before midnight. It's like driving on the left- or the right-hand side of the road, and you just can't have both. He talks about volts and amps and megawatts and windings and fork connections and legs until he has us bewildered with science.

'Will the machines be friends now?' Bríd wants to know.

He smiles and gives her a big kiss on the top of her head with his hands on the side of her face. He embraces everyone in the front room and it's time to celebrate because he's invented peace and harmony between nations. Right in the middle of the night when the whole street is asleep, he puts on music, blasting off Beethoven because he is the person who brought England and Germany back together again at Ard na Crusha, in West Clare.

So it's goodbye to the hurt mind and goodbye to the silence. Goodbye to the fear and the rules and the punishment, goodbye to guilt and shame. Goodbye to the breathing war.

Packer and I are celebrating as well. 'Goodbye to the hurt mind,' he keeps repeating out loud, on the buses, in the shops, everywhere we go, even opening the door of a pub in the daytime and shouting at the lonely drinkers inside. He even shouted it into the GPO one day at the people buying stamps and postal orders. Packer making them all look into their own hearts – bus conductors, builders, shopkeepers, men with briefcases, women with children, all staring after us with blank expressions while he laughs and leaves the words hanging in the air behind him like a long shout.

One night we met at the harbour again. He had heard about a party that was being given by one of the nurses and we were planning to gatecrash. But in order to be let in, Packer said it was not enough to arrive with beer and cigarettes. We had to come with something special. Lobster. Love and live lobster, he called it. We sat drinking one of the bottles looking out at the water which was orange and black. There was a slight fog rising over the water and the lighthouses shone a blurred, dirty light across the surface. It was calm and warm. We could hear the mullet jumping around the edge of the pier. We sat for a while, staring at the necklace of lights going all the way around the bay and at the anchored cargo ships lit up like villas in the darkness. We wondered what the sailors were doing, playing cards and waiting to unload on the docks in the city next morning. There was a foghorn, maybe the Bailey or the Kish, humming in the background. It was like the note of a church organ, a low note with no edges, coming and going again and again.

We could have gone straight to the party, but Packer

was determined to do something big, something unusual. Nothing could ever be vile and ordinary any more. We were going to arrive with something that would open everybody's eyes. The lobster storage box was padlocked, so we decided to take a boat out and get them straight from the pots. The golden handshake, Packer called it. We hid the beer beside the shed. We slipped the boat off the moorings and rowed silently out of the harbour without the noise of an engine. The tide was in and when we got to the lobster train, I held on to the oars while Packer started pulling up the ropes, examining each pot, one by one. He couldn't put his hand inside for fear of getting caught by the lobster claws, so he lifted each pot up towards the lights of the city so he could see the shape of the lobster and take it out carefully from the back.

This worked very well for the first time and we had one lobster in the boat, but when he was lifting up the next pot, Packer fell back under the weight of it. It was as if a large hand had come up from the sea and lifted him out of the boat. He disappeared without much of a splash even, down into the purple darkness with the lobster pot strapped across his chest.

I didn't know what to do. At first I thought it was funny and I imagined how Packer would be telling the heroic story later on at the party, how he nearly got himself drowned while trying to get the live lobster. I waited for him to come back up, but the water didn't move. I stood up in the boat with the oars still in my hands, but the water had become a heavy liquid, swollen like black oil. Even the ripples had disappeared and there was no chuckling under the boat. I knew Packer was being dragged all the way down to the bottom with the weight of the lobster pot across his chest and the rope fouled around his arms. I knew he was trying to free himself before it was too late, so I waited and kept the boat steady to make sure I didn't drift away.

I was the champion at staying underwater and not breathing, so I knew it was gone beyond the time that your lungs would be bursting and you would involuntarily take in water. I was watching my friend Packer drowning silently, right underneath me in the darkness. I wanted to shout, but I felt my breathing going short. I thought of jumping in after him but I would see nothing in the dark. I remembered how I once felt I was drowning, how Packer stopped talking to me and I didn't want the same thing to be happening to him. I thought of Tyrone and how he drowned all alone with the ropes wound around his legs and arms. I imagined how Packer and Tyrone would meet each other underwater, with Packer still trying to get away from the ropes and Tyrone drifting towards him with a green face and sandy hair waving, dark eyes and mouth open. Tyrone lunging at him through the water with a bottle in his hand, as if he could not bear to die alone and wanted to hold on to Packer, as if each person who drowns has the need to drag somebody else down with them to the same place, like a chain of lobster pots, one after the other, lying among the seaweed at the bottom of the sea.

'Packer,' I called out.

I thought of how they would be sending divers down to take up his body, how I would have to show them the exact spot. I thought of how they would say Packer was duplicating the tragedy of Tyrone, their faces both scarred and partially eaten by crabs. I listened to the low sound of the foghorn from the main harbour and thought this was the end. If Packer didn't come up, I would have to go down and drown with him. And when I heard him coming up to the surface behind me, I thought I could not trust life and death any more. I could see his head out of the water and hear him gasping. I saw him lashing out with his arms, trying to swim towards the lights on the shore as if I had abandoned him and he was left to struggle all the way back on his own.

'Here, I'm coming,' I called to him in a whispered shout.

I nearly stopped breathing myself as I rowed back over to where he was. He clung on to the stern. I rested the oars across each other down under the seat and helped to pull him in. Then he collapsed on the floor of the boat, coughing up water. He was trying to say 'Jesus' and he didn't care if the lobster was biting his leg because all he wanted was to be alive and to get air back into his lungs.

I took the oars up again and rowed back as fast as I could, gliding across the black water with Packer slumped over the side of the boat all the way, just coughing and retching like the sound of a seal barking. It was only when we got back to the pier that he finally picked himself up and climbed the steel ladder on the harbour wall. He staggered on his legs and bent down with his hands on his knees. I tied the rope to the ladder and followed him up quickly, feeling the cold bars in my hands. We stood on the pier as though we had both been saved.

'Jesus,' Packer said, as if it was his only word left.

He came over and put his arm around me, suddenly kissing the side of my face as if to thank me for bringing him back to life. I could feel his wet clothes. I could feel his hands shaking. I could hear him rasping heavily as if he had to relearn how to breathe in the air and make it his own. I had imagined him back to life. It was the new invention, the special talent that my mother had been talking about. I had brought Packer back from the dead and it felt like I could bring others back as well, even Tyrone, even those who were dying in Northern Ireland, even those who had died in the Irish famine, or those who had been murdered in the Ukraine.

'Let out the little divileen,' Packer shouted on his first full lungful of free air.

He was laughing coughing now and I was laughing crying, both of us more alive than we had ever been before. I got the lobster out of the boat. He took a drink of beer to get the taste of salt water out of his throat. With his arm around my shoulder, we walked away from the harbour like two ghosts just back from the dead, him holding a beer and leaning on me, squelching all the way with the water in his shoes. Me half carrying him on my shoulder with the lobster in one hand and the bag of beer in the other.

We got to the party and Packer frightened everyone with the lobster and his story of near-drowning. He cooked up the lobster and told everyone that when they went into the boiling water alive, they were not screaming, only singing an Irish lament. He talked as if he was never going to get a chance to speak again, telling everyone what it was like to drown and what it was like to be brought back to life. He was making up for all the years of silence that he would have endured as a dead person if he hadn't freed himself from the lobster pot in time. I knew that drowning was like having no friends. I had kept him alive, because that was the whole idea of friendship, that he was carrying the glory and I was carrying the secret.

They made him get out of his wet clothes and offered him a girl's dressing gown with his hairy legs sticking out underneath and his tanned chest open. We drank and ate tiny offerings of lobster. Packer had his arm around one of the nurses and she was feeling his pulse to make sure he was not still shaking. Somebody put on a record of a black woman who sang in a high, wailing voice, like a slow, exhausting musical scream that went on for a long time until she eventually calmed down again at the end. I admired the life in her lungs. Later on they told me the band was Pink Floyd and I made myself remember that name. I got talking to one of the girls at the party myself and when it was time to leave, she asked me to come back for breakfast in the morning on my own so we could listen to the song again together. She looked into my eyes and told me that she was born on the same day that Stalin died. And then it was myself and Packer again, out on the empty streets with only the birds beginning to sing around us. The two of us lying on our backs with our arms and legs stretched out, right in the middle of the main road. The two of us walking back down towards the harbour as if he had to see the place one last time so that he could turn his back on it for good. He wanted to look out over the sea to watch the sun coming up. So we sat on the rocks waiting for the first glow in the sky to the east, yellow, then pink, then orange, then blue. The tide was gone out now and the shoreline looked exhausted, draped in black seaweed. We could see the curvature of the world. We could see the grass turning green on the island. The seagulls were flying overhead, hundreds of them coming up from the south and silently flying across the bay. We saw the light-houses fading away to nothing as the sun came up like a

hot coal over the horizon, and I knew that one of these
days, very soon, I would earn my own innocence.

Twenty-one

Everybody is going over to England now to work in factories. Packer and I decided to write off to some of the addresses in Norfolk, to companies like Smedleys and Ross Foods Ltd. Packer says you can work as much overtime as you like and make a packet. England is where the money is. We both get letters back from Ross Foods inviting us to work in their factory near Norwich for three months. So it's goodbye to the harbour, because we're going over to Norfolk and then we'll head down to London to do what we like with our own money. In London, we'll be free because nobody will give a damn who we are and what we do with ourselves.

When we arrive at Ross Foods we get a bed with a straw mattress which you have to beat into shape before you can lie on it. We all sleep in Nissen huts, hundreds of beds lined up on both sides under the arched roof where you can't even stand up straight at the side, only in the middle. It's very hot inside the huts, and when the sun comes up in the morning, they say, you'll boil to death in your sleep. Packer is already making jokes and entertaining everyone, saying some of the Irish lads are liquefying in the heat, like decomposing bodies.

Somebody says the Nissen huts were left over from the war, when they flew bombing missions over to Germany from air bases close by. Somebody else said it was where German prisoners of war were kept. Sometimes we can hear air force jets flying overhead, like the sound of thunder claps echoing around the flat landscape. I've never heard them before because they don't have those jet fighters in Ireland. Packer said we have De Valera and Irish neutrality to thank for that, because otherwise we would have joined NATO after the war and the West of Ireland would be full of airfields. The bogs would be buzzing with jet fighters and the seas would be full of destroyers.

Everybody is complaining and joking about the lack of sleep. Snoring neighbours. Farting friends. Smelly socks. It's become a national pastime for the Irish to complain about the raw deal they are getting from the British. They complain about the hard work, even though they love being here, making money. Some of them refer to the foremen as Brits, because they can never forget history. But we're making money and there's nothing to spend our money on, apart from Mister Kipling apple tarts in the canteen. The personnel department of Ross Foods keeps our wages safe until the day we leave.

It's very different from working at the harbour. This is a real job where the foremen wear white coats and trilby hats. You can spot them a mile away. Some of them are good fun and make jokes, while others talk like cowboys and give orders in a Norfolk accent that Packer and all the other Irish lads have started imitating. There are lots of hard men around. Shapers. Lads who don't say very much and look mean all the time, as if they've been in lots of fights and we should be afraid of them. But everybody is so bored with the mindless work of the pea factory that they all have to talk to each other in the end, just to pass the time. The women working there are mostly from Norfolk and their jobs are easy, sitting at a conveyor belt and picking out all the bad peas, throwing them on the floor so we can sweep them away. The machines do the rest. There are graders that shake all day and night, sorting out the different sizes of peas. My job is sweeping away the peas on the floor into a drain. Packer has got the job of lining big wooden bins with black plastic sacks before they are filled with peas and sent into a massive refrigeration vault. It's all easy work, but we're already dreaming about peas. I see nothing but mountains of peas in my sleep.

There's one foreman that I like because he's a little younger than the others and I see him talking to the girls sitting at the conveyor belt. He takes a brush in his hands like a guitar and starts singing: 'A whiter shade of pale', even though nobody can hear him with the noise of the machines all around him and it looks like he's got no voice. He's only miming. All the women and girls laugh silently, miming at him with their hands, throwing peas at him to shut him up. Sometimes the girls sneak up behind him and put peas down his neck, moving their hips while he's not looking.

There are a lot of Ugandans working for Ross Foods, mostly medical students from London. You don't see them in the canteen very much, because they are trying to save every penny they earn, even more than us, maybe to send money home. They don't even smoke because that's a waste of their earnings. Packer and I get talking to some of them and they tell us that Ugandan women are the best in the world at moving their hips. Ugandan women have Venus hills like no other women in the world. They want to know what Irish women are like when they move their hips, so Packer tells them that Irish women shake all day and all night like the pea graders, with breasts like the hills around Tara and Venus mounds like the Macgillycuddy Reeks. We tell them the Irish word for sex, which is *bualadh craiceann*: beating skin. Packer tells them the Irish word for prick is *deabhailín* and they tell us that the Ugandan word for bollix is Kabula.

So then the Irish lads all over the factory are calling each other Kabulas and *deabhailíns*. 'You fucking Kabula' is what you hear all the time, but they're all joking. It's the Irish way of being friendly, insulting each other. Once, one of our lads got into an argument with one of the lads from Uganda and said he would cut off his Kabula, but it came to an end very quickly when the Ugandan medical student said he would cut off the Irish lad's Kabula and stuff it down his mouth.

Another one of the Irish lads has got a job working on the weighbridge. He weighs the trucks coming in loaded with peas and weighs them going back out again empty. He's got the best job in the whole place and everybody envies him, sitting in the sun all day, smoking cigarettes and waiting for the next truck. I think everybody would prefer to be in the factory with all the other people, where the action is. But they still call him a lucky Kabula for having so little to do, even though I think he's bored stupid and lonely out there when there are no trucks coming in. At the weekend, when all the office staff have gone home, he leaves the window of the weighbridge open, so that the Ugandans can go in and call their relatives. They queue up and talk away all night to their families back home, telling them what a great place England is. Nobody has anything against England or the fact that they were colonized like the Irish. It doesn't bother them to be working for the people who occupied their country. They just think it's nice to get reparations and make free phone calls. None of the Irish guys feel like phoning home that much, only one or two of them who pretend to call their girlfriends back in Dublin, but Packer says they're probably just talking to their sisters.

This is one of the best places in the world, away from my father's rules and away from the rules of school. I'm escaping from the wardrobe at last. I've been promoted to a job as fork-lift driver, lifting pallets and stacking them up. I'm responsible for driving the big cartons full of peas into the freezer, into the antarctic. When you drive back out again it's like returning to the tropics. Sometimes Packer jumps onto the back of the fork-lift truck behind me to get a lift back to his station, and in the pallet yard outside I have races with other fork-lift truck drivers, chasing each other around like the film *Bullitt*, racing through alleys of empty pallets stacked up like skyscrapers.

The job at Ross Foods comes to an end very suddenly. Some of the people are very bored doing the same thing all day and all night, working three shifts in a row or just sleeping and working and eating apple tarts until they start going mad. Some of them decide to walk to the nearest town and see if they might be let into a pub. Packer wants to go with them, but we're on the late shift and we want to hold our fire until we get down to London. We're back in the Nissen huts trying our best to sleep on the lumpy straw mattresses when the lads come back from the pub, drunk and singing, boasting about all the girls they met and the great time they had with them. They describe their hips and keep shouting at the Ugandan lads who are all asleep.

'English women have the best hips in the world,' one of them shouts.

'Wow, man,' another one says while the Ugandans are waking up, sitting up on their elbows, blinded and bleary with sleep, begging them to switch off the lights.

'Your Kabula goes on fire just watching them,' one of the Irish lads shouts as he moves his hips.

'Shut up, you fucking Irish *deabhailíns*,' the Ugandans say. By then everybody is annoyed at being kept up. One of them has started getting sick outside the door of the barracks and everybody is moaning.

'Would you mind puking somewhere else,' Packer shouts.

You can see that young people are like old men when it comes to sleep. There is anger all over the hut after and a fight breaks out, with one of the guys in his underpants trying to expel the drunken people. Eventually they leave and go up to the weighbridge where they can drink a bit more and phone their girlfriends in the middle of the night and everybody in our hut goes back to sleep.

But it's not long before we're awake again, because one of them has come back, this time with a shovel in his hands. We can hear him shouting outside.

'You fucking British bastards.'

It's almost dawn now, and there is a terrible cracking noise. Massive holes have been stabbed through the side of the barracks and now the sun is shining in, like a new torch beam through each hole. We can hear him shouting and cursing the British, running at the Nissen hut as if he's some kind of croppy boy coming back to get revenge with a pike in his hands.

'Aaaargh,' he shouts each time like he's still in the comic books, and then he collapses with laughter.

He's made about eight or nine holes already before anyone can get out there and take the shovel off him. Two lads in underpants, one purple, one white, take the shovel into the hut and hide it under one of the beds. But the damage is done. Packer says the place looks like a fuckin' upturned colander. When the rain comes, we'll all be soaked. Outside the drunken guy finally falls down asleep in the sun until one of his mates pulls him in like a dead man.

Next day, there is a big inquiry. It's like the time I robbed the instrument of torture at school. The manager with his trilby hat comes down to inspect the damage and then calls everybody into the canteen for a general meeting where he makes a speech in his English accent. He says he's suspending all casual work until he finds out who sabotaged the hut. He doesn't seem to be that angry, just disappointed. He says he cannot have this kind of destruction going on and he's quite happy to fire everybody in the plant if he doesn't find out who the culprit is. The people who did it must own up. Otherwise nobody will work again and everybody goes home.

The machines in the factory continue working and the foremen do all the essential jobs that we were doing before, as if they didn't need us in the first place.

Then there is another meeting in the barracks, where the Ugandans say it's for us to sort out. They'll cut off all our Kabulas and stuff them into each others' mouths if they lose their jobs. It's an Anglo-Irish problem and they should be left out of it, everyone agrees. Everybody starts discussing what to do. But the drunken vandal who did all the damage wants to stay, along with his friends. He's at university and he needs to work right to the end of the pea harvest so he can get enough money to keep himself through the year, like the Ugandan medical students. So the drunken lads who caused all the trouble have a great plan. They ask if anyone would like to volunteer, to become a paid scapegoat. They intend to make a collection which would pay for the repair of the hut as well as giving the scapegoat a huge bonus as well.

Everybody is talking about it all morning, but nobody really wants to go home. And then Packer asks me if I would like to volunteer with him. He mentions the money we would be getting and how we could be on the train later on that same evening. I tell him I like the work at Ross Foods and I would rather stay. I never want to go home again, because here I can just be myself, a fork-lift truck driver. But Packer says we can feck off down to London, and there's a rock concert coming up in Reading. We could be listening to Pink Floyd instead of working with peas. All we have to do is act the criminals for a few minutes, look guilty and contrite, say we're sorry and it will never happen again.

We are sitting in the manager's office. He's sitting behind his desk with his trilby hat resting on a stack of papers in front of him and a red ring around his forehead where the hat made an impression. First of all, he says he's glad that we owned up to the crime. He lets us know how much we will have to pay to repair the damage, but none of that worries us because we'll get all of that back with bonuses. He tells us that we will never be invited to work at Ross Foods again as long as we live, but that doesn't worry us either, because there's plenty of work to be found in England and I'm already thinking I'll get a job in a bar, or on the buses, or better still in a cinema where I can get in to see the films for free.

I tell myself this will be over soon. It's just a formality.

Embarrassing as it is, the manager will soon have to give us our money and throw us out. But then he leans back in his chair, staring at us for a long time, fixing on Packer and then fixing on me as if he's not quite finished with us. I can't look him in the eyes because I feel guilty. He's one of the nice people and I talked to him once when he came around inspecting the factory, asking me what I was going to do with my life and laughing when I said I didn't know.

Now he's staring into my eyes, like a magnifying glass burning a blade of grass in the sunlight.

'I didn't expect this from you,' he says.

'I'm sorry,' is all I can say in reply.

'But why?' he asks. 'Why did you do it?'

Packer tries to brazen it out, shrugging his shoulders. He's more defiant and therefore actually looks like he damaged the hut intentionally. Maybe I'm still resisting guilt. The manager seems unwilling to let us go without getting some kind of an answer, something that will undo the offence of this vandalism, as if the money to repair the hut is not enough without some kind of an explanation.

I have to imagine that I was the person who carried out the crime. Unlike the trial in school around the instrument of torture, this time I have to pretend I'm guilty. I tell him that we were drunk in town and that we don't know what came over us. But then he wants to know what pub we went to and what we drank. We don't know the name of the pub and he asks so many questions in rapid succession that I am in danger of giving myself away.

It's like an interrogation, only the other way around. It's become tortuous, sitting there in his office pretending to be guilty, afraid that any minute he will find out that we're innocent, afraid that I will blow it all and retract my own confession. It's like a trial in reverse. Except that when you're guilty you can put your hand up and own up to it. Go on, put me in prison. Execute me, whatever. If you're guilty, you can come clean, acknowledge your crime and take the punishment.

'Is it something you have against the British?' he asks.

'No,' Packer and I both say at the same time. 'No, it's nothing like that, honestly.'

The manager is after the truth. He wants justice. He's like a judge waiting to announce the sentence and I wonder about the whole idea of taking on guilt that doesn't belong to me. I am reminded of how my mother was shamed in front of the world after the war and now I'm being shamed myself. I realize how strange this is, when a person is put on trial, how the judge declares that he will never commit this crime himself. It's the judge who goes on trial. When the Nazis were put on trial at Nuremberg, the world gave an undertaking never to do the same again. When they executed Eichmann in Jerusalem, they gave an undertaking not to repeat his crimes. It's not the criminal who is on trial now but the rest of the world. It's the Nazis who have put us all on trial for eternity.

The manager stares at me like a psychologist, trying to work out what is inside my head.

'Why?' he asks one final time.

Then I can see Packer trying to think of a way out of this perpetual trial. He looks up at last and says it must have something to do with the peas.

'Too many peas,' he says.

And then I can't keep myself from laughing. I try to cover my face with my hand, and I'm waiting for Packer to say that peas are a vile and ordinary vegetable and we never want to see another pea as long as we live. The manager looks up in complete astonishment. We have become truly guilty now, laughing in the face of justice, mocking our accusers like cold-blooded criminals without an ounce of remorse or shame.

'It's not funny,' he says.

I realize that he's still got our money. So I try to stop laughing long enough so we can finish all this and get out of the office with what's left of our wages.

'That's really cheap,' he says to us, almost spitting it like an insult into our faces. 'You come in here and say you've smashed up the place and then laugh at it.'

At least he believes I'm guilty. And finally he opens the drawer to take out two envelopes. He's lost his patience and begrudgingly hands over the money.

'I can't understand you people,' he says, but we're already on the way out, down the stairs and out into the free world, innocent at last.

It's all over. We pack our bags and collect the money we're owed from the other lads who smashed up the hut. We're amazed at what we've come out with, and figure that we would have had to work for weeks to get this much. Some of the lads envy us and ask us what we're going to do and where we are thinking of going. Packer tells them we're off to the Reading rock festival. They call us 'fucking Kabulas' because they're all jealous of our free-dom. Packer tells them we're going to hang around in London for a while and we might head off to Berlin. He's heard of a ship that goes from Harwich to Hamburg every day. Germany is where the real money is, so it's goodbye to the peas and goodbye to the men in trilby hats and goodbye to all the sad Kabulas left behind in Ross Foods.

We get on the bus to Norwich. From there we get the

train to London, and soon we'll be looking at movies, drinking in bars and going to nightclubs. We're never looking back. We're lashing down to London, speeding through the flat countryside where all the peas are grown. Machines harvesting. Trucks waiting to be loaded. We're free and innocent while they are all still working. We will soon be dancing with women, while back at Ross Foods Ltd, they will be going insane with the sight of green peas all around them. They will be dreaming about peas and engines shaking without stopping all night. They'll be complaining about the smell of socks and the rain coming through the holes in the roof. They'll be dreaming about freedom. They'll be dreaming about women in white coats and white underwear dancing around and throwing peas at each other. They'll be dreaming about hips and Venus hills. Of peas and nipples and arms and legs. They'll be dreaming of lying down across banks of peas with women taking off their white coats. Women whispering things that you cannot hear with the noise of the graders shaking all night. Peas rolling over soft skin. Peas running along breasts and peas rolling into belly buttons like roulette.

Twenty-two

I'm out of the wardrobe now. Packer and I came to Berlin, arriving on the boat in Hamburg and coming down on the train late at night. We found jobs easily and I've started working in the store room of a publishing house. There are lots of new things happening here and it's like living in the middle of a revolution, everything rushing forward into the future, like the traffic.

When you're young, you can change your identity. You can escape from your family and change your name, leave your country, go to live in a new city and not tell anyone where you come from. You can disguise yourself like an actor and choose what to remember and what to forget. But there is always something that gives you away, some tell-tale part of you that cannot be hidden. It's not just the obvious things like your accent, your language, your appearance. It's the way you look at the world, your point of view. You can never disguise that because it shows up like ancient ruins on the landscape.

On my way to work every day I pass by the bombed-out ruins of the Kaiser Wilhelm Memorial Church, like an archaeological site left behind in the middle of the city. You can still see the bomb damage. The windows are hollow, without glass. An empty shell, left there deliberately with all its bullet holes as a reminder of war. Close to where I work, I pass by giant furniture stores where houses once stood. There's one of those gaps in the street where a house disappeared and was never rebuilt, replaced instead by a children's playground. I can hear children's voices. Echoes of children. Even at night after dark, the ghosts of children, repairing history with sweets.

One day in a bookshop I came across some black and white pictures of the church from the time before the war when it was still intact. I realized that I was looking at the same church, but they had attached a spire that didn't belong there. I could hardly recognize it, as if they had reconstructed the Rock of Cashel or rebuilt the deserted village in Achill. I thought I was mistaken and that the pictures belonged to some other city, until I read the caption underneath – Kurfürsten Damm, with a view of the Kaiser Wilhelm Memorial Church – taken in 1925. I was uneasy, looking back at this pre-war, pre-calamity time when nothing had happened yet and the worst was still to come. It was as if I could forecast the disaster of the Hitler years without being able to stop it. I didn't trust myself and wanted to get back to the present. I walked out into the street, glad to see the Memorial Church once more with my own eyes, the same as it ever was, exactly as they had left it, a beautiful, bombed-out ruin, standing still in time.

I've got a place to live on a street called Sonnenallee, in Neukölln. There are lots of young Germans living in the apartment with me, so I begin to emphasize my Irishness, spending time with people who play Irish music in the bars at night. I'm learning to play the guitar and the tin whistle, even speaking broken German like Packer, to make sure that nobody mistakes me for a real German.

Maybe it's a kind of homesickness, something I have

inherited from my mother and my father. I'm always waiting for letters from home. One day I met an old woman standing by the rows of post-boxes in the hallway of the house on Sonnenallee, waiting for letters from far away, like myself. Some of the metal doors had been forced open. Others were full of advertising leaflets, like stuffed mouths. Through the small window in the post-box, I could see that there was no mail for me, but I went all the way down and opened the door with the key, just to be sure. I was on my way back up the stairs when the old woman spoke to me very politely, stepping into the light.

'Excuse me,' she said. 'Are you the gentleman who plays the flute so beautifully?'

'Yes,' I said. I smiled, ready to talk about Ireland. But then the friendliness in her eyes disappeared. She looked me up and down, then came forward towards the banisters.

'Listen here. If I ever hear that dreadful noise again, I'll call the police.'

Later that evening, the Germans living in the apartment with me began to discuss the whole incident in a cloud of smoke. It was like a political meeting, with an ashtray and a candle at the centre of the round table. Some of them wanted to go straight down and teach her a lesson in tolerance. They planned a demonstration on the doorstep and suggested that I should perform something right under the old woman's nose. Maybe I subconsciously thought about what she might have gone through during the war, the noise of the bombing every night, so I left it. I didn't want music to be an aggression.

In the meantime, things have begun to move on. Packer is going back to Dublin to study law and I have been thinking about going to university in Berlin. I like the idea of studying German literature, which would be impossible in Dublin, because I can never live at home again. Somebody in the apartment suggested that I could take up German citizenship. With a German-born mother, it would be no problem. I could make life easy for myself.

There was another big discussion in the apartment after that. Please don't become German, somebody started saying, with praying hands. You'll have to think like a German, sleep like a German, even breathe like a German. Others thought it would make no real difference what passport you held, because your real identity would break through sooner or later. Everybody around the table was talking about how they would like to be Irish. Some of them had already been there and they spoke about the empty landscape, the standing stones, the smell of turf smoke. They asked me for tin whistle lessons. One of the girls said she would love to learn Irish. There was silence in the room as she disclosed her most secret wish, to belong to a people who had never harmed anyone. She wanted to belong to a minority, a people who were still oppressed and had not yet achieved their independence.

Then there were lots of letters for me. The old woman hanging around the post-boxes must have been jealous. She gave me a dirty look each time I opened my box, as if I had taken up correspondence with all kinds of people just to steal her post-luck away. All she got was the usual advertising leaflets which she then redistributed into the other post-boxes. Could it be, I wondered, that she was still waiting for letters that would never arrive, from the war? In the basement of the building I once found all these numbers written up in chalk on the wall, all the times she and other inhabitants spent sheltering from the bombing.

At first my mother was puzzled and wanted to know why I suddenly needed a German passport. It was like going into exile, she said, a step that she had taken when she moved to Ireland, the same step that I made as a child, every time I went out the front door into a foreign country outside on the street where they spoke English. My father warned me about losing my nationhood, but he had nothing against the plan, because I think he had always secretly wished he was more German, whereas my mother always wished she was more Irish.

My mother sent everything – birth certificates, old passports, school reports, even an old savings book. It was obvious that she didn't want to look too closely at these things in case it would remind her of the decisions she had made in her life. She would have to think about it all over again, whether it was a mistake to move countries and leave all her family of sisters behind. It was like a leap into the unknown. All those integration problems, the moments of self-doubt. She must have put everything into an envelope very hastily to avoid remembering all of that. A number of documents arrived that were of no relevance whatsoever. Her denazification papers. Her first provisional passport, stamped by the four Allies after the war, allowing her to leave Germany. She even sent her first Irish work permit, issued in Athlone. 'This alien has permission to take up employment.' I looked at her photograph on the work permit. It was from a time before I was born. I could see by her face, even in black and white, that it was taken in summer. She wore a suit and a white blouse opened out over the collar of her jacket. She had dark curly hair and her name was Irmgard Kaiser.

I put the necessary documents into an envelope and sent it off to the relevant authorities, but then I got a letter back saying they could not proceed with my application because my mother did not hold a current German passport. So I sent her back the documents and told her that I was going to stay the way I was, speckled. How could I ask her to turn the weathervane back to Germany? Had she not made her escape to Ireland? Had she not had enough trouble changing over to my father's Irish surname: O'hUrmoltaigh, a name the shopkeepers still can't pronounce and which they have started getting around by just calling her 'Mutti'. Over the years, her German humour has mixed in with Irish humour, and she has found a place in Ireland that she can call her home.

Maybe you have to live under cover for a while before you can find your true character. Now I want to belong to the same country as Bob Dylan and Dostoevsky and Fassbinder. I want to be in the same wardrobe as John Lennon and John Hamilton, the sailors with the soft eyes. I have taken on my grandfather's identity. I have given him back his name and his life, and I walk back towards Neukölln as if the city has become a harbour. It's Berlin harbour and I can hear the sound of the sea on Sonnenallee. I can hear the sway of the tide slapping underneath the boats. I can hear the sound of oars falling into place along the seats. I can feel the touch of solid ground under my feet.